GOD'S PROMISES THROUGH CHRIST

By Kay Wheeler

Author of: **God's Answers For Your Life**
God's Gift For Mothers
Your Daily Blessings
Everyday With Jesus

PRINTED IN HONG KONG

*All Scripture Quotations are from the
King James Version of the Bible*

GOD'S PROMISES THROUGH CHRIST

By Kay Wheeler

"For all the promises of God in Him are yea, and in Him, Amen." II Cor. 1:20

Contents

Introduction

All the promises of God are made possible ONLY through Christ – from Genesis to Revelation, the Bible reflects God's plan to bless and save fallen mankind through ONE PERSON, Jesus Christ! Salvation and God's promises for every human being were to be brought forth by God's own right arm, the Lamb slain before the foundation of the world, the Alpha and the Omega, the Beginning and the Ending. As the scripture states, "That the BLESSING of Abraham might come on the Gentiles through Jesus Christ." (Galatians 3:14) Herein are the precious promises of God, made real and possible through Christ Jesus, our Lord; to Whom be glory and honor forever and ever. Amen. — *Kay Wheeler*

GOD'S PROMISES THROUGH CHRIST'S WORDS

"And the Word was made flesh, and dwelt among us, and we beheld His glory as the only begotten of the Father, full of grace and truth."

John 1:1

THE PROMISES OF RECEIVING:

ABUNDANCE
ANGEL
ASSURANCE
BLESSING
COMFORT
COUNSEL
DELIVERANCE
ETERNITY
FAITH
FELLOWSHIP
FORGIVENESS
PROVISION
REWARD
RESURRECTION
SALVATION
SECURITY
STRENGTH
TRUTH
WISDOM

GOD'S PROMISES THROUGH CHRIST'S PURPOSES

"For this purpose the Son of God was manifested, that HE might destroy the works of the devil."

I John 3:8

THE PROMISES OF OBTAINING:

ANSWERS
ATONEMENT
BLESSING
COMFORT
DELIVERANCE
FORGIVENESS
GLORIFICATION
GRACE
GUIDANCE
HEADSHIP
HEALING
JUSTICE
LIGHT
LOVE
MEDIATOR
OVERCOMING
PROPHECY
RESTORATION
RESURRECTION
SACRIFICE
SALVATION
TRUTH

GOD'S PROMISES THROUGH CHRIST'S PROVISIONS

"I can do all things through Christ which strengtheneth me."

Philippians 4:13

THE PROMISES OF RECEIVING:

ANGELS
ANOINTING
BIRTH
BLOOD
BRIGHTNESS
COMPASSION
DOMINION
FATHER
GOD
IMMORTALITY
JUDGE
KING
LAMB
LORD
LOVE
MESSIAHSHIP
POWER
PRE-EXISTENCE
PRINCE
WISDOM

God's Promises through...

CHRIST'S WORDS

God's Promises through...

CHRIST'S WORDS

"And the Word was made flesh, and dwelt among us, and we beheld His glory as the only begotten of the Father, full of grace and truth."
John 1:14

THE PROMISES OF RECEIVING:

~ *Abundance* ~

But whosoever drinketh of the water that I shall give him shall never thirst; but the water that I shall give him shall be in him a well of water springing up into everlasting life.

John 4:14

And he said unto them, Cast the net on the right side of the ship, and ye shall find. They cast therefore, and now they were not able to draw it for the multitude of fishes.

John 21:6

Now when he had left speaking, he said unto Simon, Launch out into the deep, and let down your nets for a draught.

Luke 5:4

Notwithstanding, lest we should offend them, go thou to the sea, and cast an hook, and take up the fish that first cometh up; and when thou hast opened his mouth, thou shalt find a piece of money: that take, and give unto them for me and thee.

Matthew 17:27

Therefore they gathered them together, and filled twelve baskets with the fragments of the five barley loaves, which remained over and above unto them that had eaten.

John 6:13

But he answered and said, It is written, Man shall not live by bread alone, but by every word that proceedeth out of the mouth of God.

Matthew 4:4

And Simon answering said unto him, Master, we have toiled all the night, and have taken nothing: nevertheless at thy word I will let down the net.

Luke 5:5

And when they had this done, they inclosed a great multitude of fishes: and their net brake.

Luke 5:6

And they beckoned unto their partners, which were in the other ship, that they should come and help them. And they came, and filled both the ships, so that they began to sink.

Luke 5:7

When Simon Peter saw it, he fell down at Jesus' knees, saying, Depart from me; for I am a sinful man, O Lord.

Luke 5:8

For he was astonished, and all that were with him, at the draught of the fishes which they had taken.

Luke 5:9

And so was also James, and John, the sons of Zebedee, which were partners with Simon. And Jesus said unto Simon, Fear not; from henceforth thou shalt catch men.

Luke 5:10

And when they had brought their ships to land, they forsook all, and followed him.

Luke 5:11

Then Jesus said unto them, Verily, verily, I say unto you, Moses gave you not that bread from heaven; but my Father giveth you the true bread from heaven.

John 6:32

For the bread of God is he which cometh down from heaven, and giveth life unto the world.

John 6:33

And Jesus said unto them, I am the bread of life: he that cometh to me shall never hunger; and he that believeth on me shall never thirst.

John 6:35

For every one that asketh receiveth; and he that seeketh findeth; and to him that knocketh it shall be opened.

Matthew 7:8

If ye then, being evil, know how to give good gifts unto your children, how much more shall your Father which is in heaven give good things to them that ask him?

Matthew 7:11

I am the door: by me if any man enter in, he shall be saved, and shall go in and out, and find pasture.

John 10:9

The thief cometh not, but for to steal, and to kill, and to destroy: I am come that they might have life, and that they might have it more abundantly.

John 10:10

If ye shall ask any thing in my name, I will do it.

John 14:14

And these are they which are sown on good ground; such as hear the word, and receive it, and bring forth fruit, some thirtyfold, some sixty, and some an hundred.

Mark 4:20

~ *Angel* ~

He that overcometh, the same shall be clothed in white raiment; and I will not blot out his name out of the book of life, but I will confess his name before my Father, and before his angels.

Revelation 3:5

Take heed that ye despise not one of these little ones; for I say unto you, That in heaven their angels do always behold the face of my Father which is in heaven.

Matthew 18:10

Bless the LORD, ye his angels, that excel in strength, that do his commandments, hearkening unto the voice of his word.

Psalms 103:20

So shall it be at the end of the world: the angels shall come forth, and sever the wicked from among the just.

Matthew 13:49

For the Son of man shall come in the glory of his Father with his angels; and then he shall reward every man according to his works.

Matthew 16:27

And he shall send his angels with a great sound of a trumpet, and they shall gather together his elect from the four winds, from one end of heaven to the other.

Matthew 24:31

When the Son of man shall come in his glory, and all the holy angels with him, then shall he sit upon the throne of his glory.

Matthew 25:31

Thinkest thou that I cannot now pray to my Father, and he shall presently give me more than twelve legions of angels?

Matthew 26:53

And it came to pass, that the beggar died, and was carried by the angels into Abraham's bosom: the rich man also died, and was buried.

Luke 16:22

And seeth two angels in white sitting, the one at the head, and the other at the feet, where the body of Jesus had lain.

John 20:12

~ *Assurance* ~

I will not leave you comfortless: I will come to you.
John 14:18

For every one that asketh receiveth; and he that seeketh findeth; and to him that knocketh it shall be opened.

Matthew 7:8

Teaching them to observe all things whatsoever I have commanded you: and, lo, I am with you always, even unto the end of the world. Amen.
Matthew 28:20

My Father, which gave them me, is greater than all; and no man is able to pluck them out of my Father's hand.

John 10:29

While I was with them in the world, I kept them in thy name: those that thou gavest me I have kept, and none of them is lost, but the son of perdition; that the scripture might be fulfilled.

John 17:12

I am the good shepherd, and know my sheep, and am known of mine.

John 10:14

Come unto me, all ye that labour and are heavy laden, and I will give you rest.

Matthew 11:28

Take my yoke upon you, and learn of me; for I am meek and lowly in heart: and ye shall find rest unto your souls.

Matthew 11:29

For my yoke is easy, and my burden is light.

Matthew 11:30

And I will pray the Father, and he shall give you another Comforter, that he may abide with you for ever.

John 14:16

Even the Spirit of truth; whom the world cannot receive, because it seeth him not, neither knoweth him: but ye know him; for he dwelleth with you, and shall be in you.

John 14:17

Then spake Jesus again unto them, saying, I am the light of the world: he that followeth me shall not walk in darkness, but shall have the light of life.

John 8:12

And ye shall be betrayed both by parents, and brethren, and kinsfolks, and friends; and some of you shall they cause to be put to death.

Luke 21:16

And ye shall be hated of all men for my name's sake.

Luke 21:17

But there shall not an hair of your head perish.

Luke 21:18

And the peace of God, which passeth all understanding, shall keep your hearts and minds through Christ Jesus.

Philippians 4:7

~ *Blessing* ~

Blessed are the poor in spirit: for theirs is the kingdom of heaven.

Matthew 5:3

Blessed are they that mourn: for they shall be comforted.

Matthew 5:4

Blessed are the meek: for they shall inherit the earth.

Matthew 5:5

Blessed are they which do hunger and thirst after righteousness: for they shall be filled.

Matthew 5:6

Blessed are the merciful: for they shall obtain mercy.

Matthew 5:7

Blessed are the pure in heart: for they shall see God.

Matthew 5:8

Blessed are the peacemakers: for they shall be called the children of God.

Matthew 5:9

Blessed are those servants, whom the lord when he cometh shall find watching: verily I say unto you, that he shall gird himself, and make them to sit down to meat, and will come forth and serve them.

Luke 12:37

And if he shall come in the second watch, or come in the third watch, and find them so, blessed are those servants.

Luke 12:38

His lord said unto him, Well done, thou good and faithful servant: thou hast been faithful over a few things, I will make thee ruler over many things: enter thou into the joy of thy lord.

Matthew 25:21

These things have I spoken unto you, that my joy might remain in you, and that your joy might be full.

John 15:11

Then shall the King say unto them on his right hand, Come, ye blessed of my Father, inherit the kingdom prepared for you from the foundation of the world.

Matthew 25:34

Then shall the righteous shine forth as the sun in the kingdom of their Father. Who hath ears to hear, let him hear.

Matthew 13:43

If ye then, being evil, know how to give good gifts unto your children, how much more shall your Father which is in heaven give good things to them that ask him?

Matthew 7:11

Verily, verily, I say unto you, He that believeth on me hath everlasting life.

John 6:47

Then spake Jesus again unto them, saying, I am the light of the world: he that followeth me shall not walk in darkness, but shall have the light of life.

John 8:12

And Jesus answered and said, Verily I say unto you, There is no man that hath left house, or brethren, or sisters, or father, or mother, or wife, or children, or lands, for my sake, and the gospel's,

Mark 10:29

But he shall receive an hundredfold now in this time, houses, and brethren, and sisters, and mothers, and children, and lands, with persecutions; and in the world to come eternal life.

Mark 10:30

But he said, Yea rather, blessed are they that hear the word of God, and keep it.

Luke 11:28

And I say unto you, Ask, and it shall be given you; seek, and ye shall find; knock, and it shall be opened unto you.

Luke 11:9

Blessed be the God and Father of our Lord Jesus Christ, who hath blessed us with all spiritual blessings in heavenly places in Christ.

Ephesians 1:3

~ *Comfort* ~

I will not leave you comfortless: I will come to you.

John 14:18

If ye then, being evil, know how to give good gifts unto your children, how much more shall your Father which is in heaven give good things to them that ask him?

Matthew 7:11

For where two or three are gathered together in my name, there am I in the midst of them.

Matthew 18:20

He that hath an ear, let him hear what the Spirit saith unto the churches; To him that overcometh will I give to eat of the hidden manna, and will give him a white stone, and in the stone a new name written, which no man knoweth saving he that receiveth it.

Revelation 2:17

And I will give him the morning star.

Revelation 2:28

...The LORD is my shepherd; I shall not want.

Psalms 23:1

He maketh me to lie down in green pastures: he leadeth me beside the still waters.

Psalms 23:2

He restoreth my soul: he leadeth me in the paths of righteousness for his name's sake.

Psalms 23:3

I am come a light into the world, that whosoever believeth on me should not abide in darkness.

John 12:46

In a little wrath I hid my face from thee for a moment; but with everlasting kindness will I have mercy on thee, saith the LORD thy Redeemer.

Isaiah 54:8

But after that the kindness and love of God our Saviour toward man appeared.

Titus 3:4

Not by works of righteousness which we have done, but according to his mercy he saved us, by the washing of regeneration, and renewing of the Holy Ghost.

Titus 3:5

For the Lamb which is in the midst of the throne shall feed them, and shall lead them unto living fountains of waters: and God shall wipe away all tears from their eyes.

Revelation 7:17

For unto us a child is born, unto us a son is given: and the government shall be upon his shoulder: and his name shall be called Wonderful, Counsellor, The mighty God, The everlasting Father, The Prince of Peace.

Isaiah 9:6

If ye shall ask any thing in my name, I will do it.

John 14:14

And I will pray the Father, and he shall give you another Comforter, that he may abide with you for ever;

John 14:16

Even the Spirit of truth; whom the world cannot receive, because it seeth him not, neither knoweth him: but ye know him; for he dwelleth with you, and shall be in you.

John 14:17

But the Comforter, which is the Holy Ghost, whom the Father will send in my name, he shall teach you all things, and bring all things to your remembrance, whatsoever I have said unto you.

John 14:26

And the peace of God, which passeth all understanding, shall keep your hearts and minds through Christ Jesus.

Philippians 4:7

These things I have spoken unto you, that in me ye might have peace. In the world ye shall have tribulation: but be of good cheer; I have overcome the world.

John 16:33

Peace I leave with you, my peace I give unto you: not as the world giveth, give I unto you. Let not your heart be troubled, neither let it be afraid.

John 14:27

To proclaim the acceptable year of the LORD, and the day of vengeance of our God; to comfort all that mourn.

Isaiah 61:2

~ Counsel ~

He that believeth on me, as the scripture hath said, out of his belly shall flow rivers of living water.

John 7:38

Thus saith the LORD, thy Redeemer, the Holy One of Israel; I am the LORD thy God which teacheth thee to profit, which leadeth thee by the way that thou shouldest go.

Isaiah 48:17

Therefore take no thought, saying, What shall we eat? or, What shall we drink? or, Wherewithal shall we be clothed?

Matthew 6:31

(For after all these things do the Gentiles seek:) for your heavenly Father knoweth that ye have need of all these things.

Matthew 6:32

But seek ye first the kingdom of God, and his righteousness; and all these things shall be added unto you.

Matthew 6:33

Take therefore no thought for the morrow: for the morrow shall take thought for the things of itself. Sufficient unto the day is the evil thereof.

Matthew 6:34

Beware of false prophets, which come to you in sheep's clothing, but inwardly they are ravening wolves.

Matthew 7:15

Ye shall know them by their fruits. Do men gather grapes of thorns, or figs of thistles?

Matthew 7:16

Even so every good tree bringeth forth good fruit; but a corrupt tree bringeth forth evil fruit.

Matthew 7:17

No man can serve two masters: for either he will hate the one, and love the other; or else he will hold to the one, and despise the other. Ye cannot serve God and mammon.

Matthew 6:24

And take heed to yourselves, lest at any time your hearts be overcharged with surfeiting, and drunkenness, and cares of this life, and so that day come upon you unawares.

Luke 21:34

And he said unto them, Take heed, and beware of covetousness: for a man's life consisteth not in the abundance of the things which he possesseth.

Luke 12:15

Wherefore if thy hand or thy foot offend thee, cut them off, and cast them from thee: it is better for thee to enter into life halt or maimed, rather than having two hands or two feet to be cast into everlasting fire.

Matthew 18:8

And if thine eye offend thee, pluck it out, and cast it from thee: it is better for thee to enter into life with one eye, rather than having two eyes to be cast into hell fire.

Matthew 18:9

Judge not, that ye be not judged.

Matthew 7:1

For with what judgment ye judge, ye shall be judged: and with what measure ye mete, it shall be measured to you again.

Matthew 7:2

And why beholdest thou the mote that is in thy brother's eye, but considerest not the beam that is in thine own eye?

Matthew 7:3

Or how wilt thou say to thy brother, Let me pull out the mote out of thine eye; and, behold, a beam is in thine own eye?

Matthew 7:4

Thou hypocrite, first cast out the beam out of thine own eye; and then shalt thou see clearly to cast out the mote out of thy brother's eye.

Matthew 7:5

Give not that which is holy unto the dogs, neither cast ye your pearls before swine, lest they trample them under their feet, and turn again and rend you.

Matthew 7:6

And Jesus answered and said unto them, Take heed that no man deceive you.

Matthew 24:4

For many shall come in my name, saying, I am Christ; and shall deceive many.

Matthew 24:5

And ye shall hear of wars and rumours of wars: see that ye be not troubled: for all these things must come to pass, but the end is not yet.

Matthew 24:6

For nation shall rise against nation, and kingdom against kingdom: and there shall be famines, and pestilences, and earthquakes, in divers places.

Matthew 24:7

All these are the beginning of sorrows.

Matthew 24:8

Then shall they deliver you up to be afflicted, and shall kill you: and ye shall be hated of all nations for my name's sake.

Matthew 24:9

And then shall many be offended, and shall betray one another, and shall hate one another.

Matthew 24:10

And many false prophets shall rise, and shall deceive many.

Matthew 24:11

And because iniquity shall abound, the love of many shall wax cold.

Matthew 24:12

But he that shall endure unto the end, the same shall be saved.

Matthew 24:13

Then said Jesus unto him, Put up again thy sword into his place: for all they that take the sword shall perish with the sword.

Matthew 26:52

But I say unto you, That ye resist not evil: but whosoever shall smite thee on thy right cheek, turn to him the other also.

Matthew 5:39

And if any man will sue thee at the law, and take away thy coat, let him have thy cloke also.

Matthew 5:40

And whosoever shall compel thee to go a mile, go with him twain.

Matthew 5:41

~ *Deliverance* ~

And ye shall know the truth, and the truth shall make you free.

John 8:32

They answered him, We be Abraham's seed, and were never in bondage to any man: how sayest thou, Ye shall be made free?

John 8:33

Jesus answered them, Verily, verily, I say unto you, Whosoever committeth sin is the servant of sin.

John 8:34

And the servant abideth not in the house for ever: but the Son abideth ever.

John 8:35

If the Son therefore shall make you free, ye shall be free indeed.

John 8:36

Their Redeemer is strong; the LORD of hosts is his name: he shall throughly plead their cause, that he may give rest to the land, and disquiet the inhabitants of Babylon.

Jeremiah 50:34

And it shall be for a sign and for a witness unto the LORD of hosts in the land of Egypt: for they shall cry unto the LORD because of the oppressors, and he shall send them a saviour, and a great one, and he shall deliver them.

Isaiah 19:20

For the Lamb which is in the midst of the throne shall feed them, and shall lead them unto living fountains of waters: and God shall wipe away all tears from their eyes.

Revelation 7:17

And there shall be no more curse: but the throne of God and of the Lamb shall be in it; and his servants shall serve him.

Revelation 22:3

Surely he hath borne our griefs, and carried our sorrows: yet we did esteem him stricken, smitten of God, and afflicted.

Isaiah 53:4

Even as the Son of man came not to be ministered unto, but to minister, and to give his life a ransom for many.

Matthew 20:28

Notwithstanding the Lord stood with me, and strengthened me; that by me the preaching might be fully known, and that all the Gentiles might hear: and I was delivered out of the mouth of the lion.

II Timothy 4:17

And the Lord shall deliver me from every evil work, and will preserve me unto his heavenly kingdom: to whom be glory for ever and ever. Amen.

II Timothy 4:18

And there arose a great storm of wind, and the waves beat into the ship, so that it was now full.

Mark 4:37

And he was in the hinder part of the ship, asleep on a pillow: and they awake him, and say unto him, Master, carest thou not that we perish?

Mark 4:38

And he arose, and rebuked the wind, and said unto the sea, Peace, be still. And the wind ceased, and there was a great calm.

Mark 4:39

The spirit of the Lord GOD is upon me; because the LORD hath anointed me to preach good tidings unto the meek; he hath sent me to bind up the brokenhearted, to proclaim liberty to the captives, and the opening of the prison to them that are bound.

Isaiah 61:1

But if I with the finger of God cast out devils, no doubt the kingdom of God is come upon you.

Luke 11:20

~ Eternity ~

Verily, verily, I say unto you, If a man keep my saying, he shall never see death.

John 8:51

But is now made manifest by the appearing of our Saviour Jesus Christ, who hath abolished death, and hath brought life and immortality to light through the gospel.

II Timothy 1:10

For so an entrance shall be ministered unto you abundantly into the everlasting kingdom of our Lord and Saviour Jesus Christ.

II Peter 1:11

For the wages of sin is death; but the gift of God is eternal life through Jesus Christ our Lord.

Romans 6:23

And when I saw him, I fell at his feet as dead. And he laid his right hand upon me, saying unto me, Fear not; I am the first and the last.

Revelation 1:17

I am he that liveth, and was dead; and, behold, I am alive for evermore, Amen; and have the keys of hell and of death.

Revelation 1:18

And I heard a great voice out of heaven saying, Behold, the tabernacle of God is with men, and he will dwell with them, and they shall be his people, and God himself shall be with them, and be their God.

Revelation 21:3

And God shall wipe away all tears from their eyes; and there shall be no more death, neither sorrow, nor crying, neither shall there be any more pain: for the former things are passed away.

Revelation 21:4

And he that sat upon the throne said, Behold, I make all things new. And he said unto me, Write: for these words are true and faithful.

Revelation 21:5

And he said unto me, It is done. I am Alpha and Omega, the beginning and the end. I will give unto him that is athirst of the fountain of the water of life freely.

Revelation 21:6

And if I go and prepare a place for you, I will come again, and receive you unto myself; that where I am, there ye may be also.

John 14:3

Verily, verily, I say unto you, He that heareth my word, and believeth on him that sent me, hath everlasting life, and shall not come into condemnation; but is passed from death unto life.

John 5:24

For God so loved the world, that he gave his only begotten Son, that whosoever believeth in him should not perish, but have everlasting life.

John 3:16

As thou hast given him power over all flesh, that he should give eternal life to as many as thou hast given him.

John 17:2

~ *Faith* ~

Looking unto Jesus the author and finisher of our faith; who for the joy that was set before him endured the cross, despising the shame, and is set down at the right hand of the throne of God.

Hebrews 12:2

That the trial of your faith, being much more precious than of gold that perisheth, though it be tried with fire, might be found unto praise and honour and glory at the appearing of Jesus Christ.

I Peter 1:7

Jesus said unto him, If thou canst believe, all things are possible to him that believeth.

Mark 9:23

Therefore being justified by faith, we have peace with God through our Lord Jesus Christ:

Romans 5:1

By whom also we have access by faith into this grace wherein we stand, and rejoice in hope of the glory of God.

Romans 5:2

And be found in him, not having mine own righteousness, which is of the law, but that which is through the faith of Christ, the righteousness which is of God by faith.

Philippians 3:9

And Jesus answering saith unto them, Have faith in God.

Mark 11:22

For verily I say unto you, That whosoever shall say unto this mountain, Be thou removed, and be thou cast into the sea; and shall not doubt in his heart, but shall believe that those things which he saith shall come to pass; he shall have whatsoever he saith.

Mark 11:23

And Jesus said unto them, Because of your unbelief: for verily I say unto you, If ye have faith as a grain of mustard seed, ye shall say unto this mountain, Remove hence to yonder place; and it shall remove; and nothing shall be impossible unto you.

Matthew 17:20

And he said unto him, Arise, go thy way: thy faith hath made thee whole.

Luke 17:19

Then Jesus answered and said unto her, O woman, great is thy faith: be it unto thee even as thou wilt. And her daughter was made whole from that very hour.

Matthew 15:28

And he said to the woman, Thy faith hath saved thee; go in peace.

Luke 7:50

But when Jesus heard it, he answered him, saying, Fear not: believe only, and she shall be made whole.

Luke 8:50

And now I have told you before it come to pass, that, when it is come to pass, ye might believe.

John 14:29

Paul, an apostle of Jesus Christ by the commandment of God our Saviour, and Lord Jesus Christ, which is our hope.

I Timothy 1:1

For we are saved by hope: but hope that is seen is not hope: for what a man seeth, why doth he yet hope for?

Romans 8:24

Take therefore no thought for the morrow: for the morrow shall take thought for the things of itself. Sufficient unto the day is the evil thereof.

Matthew 6:34

But straightway Jesus spake unto them, saying, Be of good cheer; it is I; be not afraid.

Matthew 14:27

And Jesus came and touched them, and said, Arise, and be not afraid.

Matthew 17:7

Now our Lord Jesus Christ himself, and God, even our Father, which hath loved us, and hath given us everlasting consolation and good hope through grace.

II Thessalonians 2:16

~ *Fellowship* ~

Then said Jesus to those Jews which believed on him, If ye continue in my word, then are ye my disciples indeed.

John 8:31

He that eateth my flesh, and drinketh my blood, dwelleth in me, and I in him.

John 6:56

Jesus answered and said unto him, If a man love me, he will keep my words: and my Father will love him, and we will come unto him, and make our abode with him.

John 14:23

For thy Maker is thine husband; the LORD of hosts is his name; and thy Redeemer the Holy One of Israel; The God of the whole earth shall he be called.

Isaiah 54:5

Doubtless thou art our father, though Abraham be ignorant of us, and Israel acknowledge us not: thou, O LORD, art our father, our redeemer; thy name is from everlasting.

Isaiah 63:16

And my spirit hath rejoiced in God my Saviour.

Luke 1:47

Also I say unto you, Whosoever shall confess me before men, him shall the Son of man also confess before the angels of God.

Luke 12:8

Ye are my friends, if ye do whatsoever I command you.

John 15:14

For ye are all the children of God by faith in Christ Jesus.

Galatians 3:26

For as many of you as have been baptized into Christ have put on Christ.

Galatians 3:27

There is neither Jew nor Greek, there is neither bond nor free, there is neither male nor female: for ye are all one in Christ Jesus.

Galatians 3:28

But if we walk in the light, as he is in the light, we have fellowship one with another, and the blood of Jesus Christ his Son cleanseth us from all sin.

I John 1:7

For, brethren, ye have been called unto liberty; only use not liberty for an occasion to the flesh, but by love serve one another.

Galatians 5:13

Behold, I stand at the door, and knock: if any man hear my voice, and open the door, I will come in to him, and will sup with him, and he with me.

Revelation 3:20

Now ye are the body of Christ, and members in particular.

I Corinthians 12:27

God is faithful, by whom ye were called unto the fellowship of his Son Jesus Christ our Lord.

I Corinthians 1:9

Now I beseech you, brethren, by the name of our Lord Jesus Christ, that ye all speak the same thing, and that there be no divisions among you; but that ye be perfectly joined together in the same mind and in the same judgment.

I Corinthians 1:10

Neither pray I for these alone, but for them also which shall believe on me through their word;

John 17:20

That they all may be one; as thou, Father, art in me, and I in thee, that they also may be one in us: that the world may believe that thou hast sent me.

John 17:21

And the glory which thou gavest me I have given them; that they may be one, even as we are one:

John 17:22

I in them, and thou in me, that they may be made perfect in one; and that the world may know that thou hast sent me, and hast loved them, as thou hast loved me.

John 17:23

And he stretched forth his hand toward his disciples, and said, Behold my mother and my brethren!

Matthew 12:49

For whosoever shall do the will of my Father which is in heaven, the same is my brother, and sister, and mother.

Matthew 12:50

At that day ye shall know that I am in my Father, and ye in me, and I in you.

John 14:20

~ *Forgiveness* ~

In a little wrath I hid my face from thee for a moment; but with everlasting kindness will I have mercy on thee, saith the LORD thy Redeemer.

Isaiah 54:8

Him hath God exalted with his right hand to be a Prince and a Saviour, for to give repentance to Israel, and forgiveness of sins.

Acts 5:31

And not only so, but we also joy in God through our Lord Jesus Christ, by whom we have now received the atonement.

Romans 5:11

But that ye may know that the Son of man hath power on earth to forgive sins, (he saith to the sick of the palsy,).

Mark 2:10

If we confess our sins, he is faithful and just to forgive us our sins, and to cleanse us from all unrighteousness.

I John 1:9

For by grace are ye saved through faith; and that not of yourselves: it is the gift of God.

Ephesians 2:8

Not of works, lest any man should boast.

Ephesians 2:9

For we are his workmanship, created in Christ Jesus unto good works, which God hath before ordained that we should walk in them.

Ephesians 2:10

In whom we have redemption through his blood, the forgiveness of sins, according to the riches of his grace.

Ephesians 1:7

For where two or three are gathered together in my name, there am I in the midst of them.

Matthew 18:20

Then came Peter to him, and said, Lord, how oft shall my brother sin against me, and I forgive him? till seven times?

Matthew 18:21

Jesus saith unto him, I say not unto thee, Until seven times: but, Until seventy times seven.

Matthew 18:22

Then said Jesus, Father, forgive them; for they know not what they do. And they parted his raiment, and cast lots.

Luke 23:34

And when ye stand praying, forgive, if ye have ought against any: that your Father also which is in heaven may forgive you your trespasses.

Mark 11:25

~ *Provision* ~

Therefore I say unto you, What things soever ye desire, when ye pray, believe that ye receive them, and ye shall have them.

Mark 11:24

And in that day ye shall ask me nothing. Verily, verily, I say unto you, Whatsoever ye shall ask the Father in my name, he will give it you.

John 16:23

And he said unto me, My grace is sufficient for thee: for my strength is made perfect in weakness. Most gladly therefore will I rather glory in my infirmities, that the power of Christ may rest upon me.

II Corinthians 12:9

And all things, whatsoever ye shall ask in prayer, believing, ye shall receive.

Matthew 21:22

He that spared not his own Son, but delivered him up for us all, how shall he not with him also freely give us all things?

Romans 8:32

Blessed are they which do hunger and thirst after righteousness: for they shall be filled.

Matthew 5:6

Thus saith the LORD, thy Redeemer, the Holy One of Israel; I am the LORD thy God which teacheth thee to profit, which leadeth thee by the way that thou shouldest go.

Isaiah 48:17

He shall see of the travail of his soul, and shall be satisfied: by his knowledge shall my righteous servant justify many; for he shall bear their iniquities.

Isaiah 53:11

But I am poor and needy; yet the Lord thinketh upon me: thou art my help and my deliverer; make no tarrying, O my God.

Psalms 40:17

And he said unto his disciples, Therefore I say unto you, Take no thought for your life, what ye shall eat; neither for the body, what ye shall put on.

Luke 12:22

The life is more than meat, and the body is more than raiment.

Luke 12:23

Consider the ravens: for they neither sow nor reap; which neither have storehouse nor barn; and God feedeth them: how much more are ye better than the fowls?

Luke 12:24

I know both how to be abased, and I know how to abound: every where and in all things I am instructed both to be full and to be hungry, both to abound and to suffer need.

Philippians 4:12

I can do all things through Christ which strengtheneth me.

Philippians 4:13

But my God shall supply all your need according to his riches in glory by Christ Jesus.

Philippians 4:19

But seek ye first the kingdom of God, and his righteousness; and all these things shall be added unto you.

Matthew 6:33

And Jesus said unto them, I am the bread of life: he that cometh to me shall never hunger; and he that believeth on me shall never thirst.

John 6:35

And ye are complete in him, which is the head of all principality and power.

Colossians 2:10

~ *Reward* ~

For the Son of man shall come in the glory of his Father with his angels; and then he shall reward every man according to his works.

Matthew 16:27

Then shall the King say unto them on his right hand, Come, ye blessed of my Father, inherit the kingdom prepared for you from the foundation of the world:

Matthew 25:34

For every one that asketh receiveth; and he that seeketh findeth; and to him that knocketh it shall be opened.

Luke 11:10

If a son shall ask bread of any of you that is a father, will he give him a stone? or if he ask a fish, will he for a fish give him a serpent?

Luke 11:11

Or if he shall ask an egg, will he offer him a scorpion?

Luke 11:12

If ye then, being evil, know how to give good gifts unto your children: how much more shall your heavenly Father give the Holy Spirit to them that ask him?

Luke 11:13

To him that overcometh will I grant to sit with me in my throne, even as I also overcame, and am set down with my Father in his throne.

Revelation 3:21

His lord said unto him, Well done, thou good and faithful servant: thou hast been faithful over a few things, I will make thee ruler over many things: enter thou into the joy of thy lord.

Matthew 25:21

And the Lord said, Who then is that faithful and wise steward, whom his lord shall make ruler over his household, to give them their portion of meat in due season?

Luke 12:42

Blessed is that servant, whom his lord when he cometh shall find so doing.

Luke 12:43

Of a truth I say unto you, that he will make him ruler over all that he hath.

Luke 12:44

And when thou prayest, thou shalt not be as the hypocrites are: for they love to pray standing in the synagogues and in the corners of the streets, that they may be seen of men. Verily I say unto you, They have their reward.

Matthew 6:5

But thou, when thou prayest, enter into thy closet, and when thou hast shut thy door, pray to thy Father which is in secret; and thy Father which seeth in secret shall reward thee openly.

Matthew 6:6

Blessed are ye, when men shall hate you, and when they shall separate you from their company, and shall reproach you, and cast out your name as evil, for the Son of man's sake.

Luke 6:22

Rejoice ye in that day, and leap for joy: for, behold, your reward is great in heaven: for in the like manner did their fathers unto the prophets.

Luke 6:23

He that overcometh, the same shall be clothed in white raiment; and I will not blot out his name out of the book of life, but I will confess his name before my Father, and before his angels.

Revelation 3:5

Because thou hast kept the word of my patience, I also will keep thee from the hour of temptation, which shall come upon all the world, to try them that dwell upon the earth.

Revelation 3:10

Him that overcometh will I make a pillar in the temple of my God, and he shall go no more out: and I will write upon him the name of my God, and the name of the city of my God, which is new Jerusalem, which cometh down out of heaven from my God: and I will write upon him my new name.

Revelation 3:12

And he said unto me, It is done. I am Alpha and Omega, the beginning and the end. I will give unto him that is athirst of the fountain of the water of life freely.

Revelation 21:6

He that overcometh shall inherit all things; and I will be his God, and he shall be my son.

Revelation 21:7

And, behold, I come quickly; and my reward is with me, to give every man according as his work shall be.

Revelation 22:12

I am Alpha and Omega, the beginning and the end, the first and the last.

Revelation 22:13

Take heed that ye do not your alms before men, to be seen of them: otherwise ye have no reward of your Father which is in heaven.

Matthew 6:1

Therefore when thou doest thine alms, do not sound a trumpet before thee, as the hypocrites do in the synagogues and in the streets, that they may have glory of men. Verily I say unto you, They have their reward.

Matthew 6:2

But when thou doest alms, let not thy left hand know what thy right hand doeth.

Matthew 6:3

That thine alms may be in secret: and thy Father which seeth in secret himself shall reward thee openly.

Matthew 6:4

And whosoever shall give to drink unto one of these little ones a cup of cold water only in the name of a disciple, verily I say unto you, he shall in no wise lose his reward.

Matthew 10:42

In my Father's house are many mansions: if it were not so, I would have told you. I go to prepare a place for you.

John 14:2

~ *Resurrection* ~

Whoso eateth my flesh, and drinketh my blood, hath eternal life; and I will raise him up at the last day.

John 6:54

Verily, verily, I say unto you, If a man keep my saying, he shall never see death.

John 8:51

For I know that my redeemer liveth, and that he shall stand at the latter day upon the earth.

Job 19:25

All that the Father giveth me shall come to me; and him that cometh to me I will in no wise cast out.

John 6:37

And this is the will of him that sent me, that every one which seeth the Son, and believeth on him, may have everlasting life: and I will raise him up at the last day.

John 6:40

No man can come to me, except the Father which hath sent me draw him: and I will raise him up at the last day.

John 6:44

It is written in the prophets, And they shall be all taught of God. Every man therefore that hath heard, and hath learned of the Father, cometh unto me.

John 6:45

Not that any man hath seen the Father, save he which is of God, he hath seen the Father.

John 6:46

Verily, verily, I say unto you, He that believeth on me hath everlasting life.

John 6:47

So when this corruptible shall have put on incorruption, and this mortal shall have put on immortality, then shall be brought to pass the saying that is written, Death is swallowed up in victory.

I Corinthians 15:54

O death, where is thy sting? O grave, where is thy victory?

I Corinthians 15:55

But thanks be to God, which giveth us the victory through our Lord Jesus Christ.

I Corinthians 15:57

Verily, verily, I say unto you, He that heareth my word, and believeth on him that sent me, hath everlasting life, and shall not come into condemnation; but is passed from death unto life.

John 5:24

Verily, verily, I say unto you, The hour is coming, and now is, when the dead shall hear the voice of the Son of God: and they that hear shall live.

John 5:25

Now that the dead are raised, even Moses shewed at the bush, when he calleth the Lord the God of Abraham, and the God of Isaac, and the God of Jacob.

Luke 20:37

For he is not a God of the dead, but of the living: for all live unto him.

Luke 20:38

For as the Father raiseth up the dead, and quickeneth them; even so the Son quickeneth whom he will.

John 5:21

For I am not ashamed of the gospel of Christ: for it is the power of God unto salvation to every one that believeth; to the Jew first, and also to the Greek.

Romans 1:16

Blessed and holy is he that hath part in the first resurrection: on such the second death hath no power, but they shall be priests of God and of Christ, and shall reign with him a thousand years.

Revelation 20:6

~ *Salvation* ~

The next day John seeth Jesus coming unto him, and saith, Behold the Lamb of God, which taketh away the sin of the world.

John 1:29

And Abraham said, My son, God will provide himself a lamb for a burnt offering: so they went both of them together.

Genesis 22:8

But he was wounded for our transgressions, he was bruised for our iniquities: the chastisement of our peace was upon him; and with his stripes we are healed.

Isaiah 53:5

All we like sheep have gone astray; we have turned every one to his own way; and the LORD hath laid on him the iniquity of us all.

Isaiah 53:6

He was oppressed, and he was afflicted, yet he opened not his mouth: he is brought as a lamb to the slaughter, and as a sheep before her shearers is dumb, so he openeth not his mouth.

Isaiah 53:7

He was taken from prison and from judgment: and who shall declare his generation? for he was cut off out of the land of the living: for the transgression of my people was he stricken.

Isaiah 53:8

And he made his grave with the wicked, and with the rich in his death; because he had done no violence, neither was any deceit in his mouth.

Isaiah 53:9

Yet it pleased the LORD to bruise him; he hath put him to grief: when thou shalt make his soul an offering for sin, he shall see his seed, he shall prolong his days, and the pleasure of the LORD shall prosper in his hand.

Isaiah 53:10

And I will put enmity between thee and the woman, and between thy seed and her seed; it shall bruise thy head, and thou shalt bruise his heel.

Genesis 3:15

And for this cause he is the mediator of the new testament, that by means of death, for the redemption of the transgressions that were under the first testament, they which are called might receive the promise of eternal inheritance.

Hebrews 9:15

For the Son of man is come to save that which was lost.

Matthew 18:11

For there is one God, and one mediator between God and men, the man Christ Jesus.

I Timothy 2:5

For then must he often have suffered since the foundation of the world: but now once in the end of the world hath he appeared to put away sin by the sacrifice of himself.

Hebrews 9:26

For this is my blood of the new testament, which is shed for many for the remission of sins.

Matthew 26:28

Therefore being justified by faith, we have peace with God through our Lord Jesus Christ.

Romans 5:1

What man of you, having an hundred sheep, if he lose one of them, doth not leave the ninety and nine in the wilderness, and go after that which is lost, until he find it?

Luke 15:4

And when he hath found it, he layeth it on his shoulders, rejoicing.

Luke 15:5

And when he cometh home, he calleth together his friends and neighbours, saying unto them, Rejoice with me; for I have found my sheep which was lost.

Luke 15:6

I say unto you, that likewise joy shall be in heaven over one sinner that repenteth, more than over ninety and nine just persons, which need no repentance.

Luke 15:7

That if thou shalt confess with thy mouth the Lord Jesus, and shalt believe in thine heart that God hath raised him from the dead, thou shalt be saved.

Romans 10:9

For God so loved the world, that he gave his only begotten Son, that whosoever believeth in him should not perish, but have everlasting life.

John 3:16

Simon Peter, a servant and an apostle of Jesus Christ, to them that have obtained like precious faith with us through the righteousness of God and our Saviour Jesus Christ.

II Peter 1:1

Not by works of righteousness which we have done, but according to his mercy he saved us, by the washing of regeneration, and renewing of the Holy Ghost;

Titus 3:5

Which he shed on us abundantly through Jesus Christ our Saviour.

Titus 3:6

And we have seen and do testify that the Father sent the Son to be the Saviour of the world.

I John 4:14

For the Son of man is come to seek and to save that which was lost.

Luke 19:10

Verily, verily, I say unto you, He that believeth on me hath everlasting life.

John 6:47

Therefore if any man be in Christ, he is a new creature: old things are passed away; behold, all things are become new.

II Corinthians 5:17

Who hath saved us, and called us with an holy calling, not according to our works, but according to his own purpose and grace, which was given us in Christ Jesus before the world began.

II Timothy 1:9

~ *Security* ~

Therefore whosoever heareth these sayings of mine, and doeth them, I will liken him unto a wise man, which built his house upon a rock.

Matthew 7:24

And the rain descended, and the floods came, and the winds blew, and beat upon that house; and it fell not: for it was founded upon a rock.

Matthew 7:25

And they remembered that God was their rock, and the high God their redeemer.

Psalms 78:35

Thus saith the LORD, thy redeemer, and he that formed thee from the womb, I am the LORD that maketh all things; that stretcheth forth the heavens alone; that spreadeth abroad the earth by myself.

Isaiah 44:24

That frustrateth the tokens of the liars, and maketh diviners mad; that turneth wise men backward, and maketh their knowledge foolish.

Isaiah 44:25

That confirmeth the word of his servant, and performeth the counsel of his messengers; that saith to Jerusalem, Thou shalt be inhabited; and to the cities of Judah, Ye shall be built, and I will raise up the decayed places thereof.

Isaiah 44:26

That saith to the deep, Be dry, and I will dry up thy rivers.

Isaiah 44:27

Thou shalt also suck the milk of the Gentiles, and shalt suck the breast of kings: and thou shalt know that I the LORD am thy Saviour and thy Redeemer, the mighty One of Jacob.

Isaiah 44:27

For in him we live, and move, and have our being; as certain also of your own poets have said, For we are also his offspring.

Acts 17:28

And the peace of God, which passeth all understanding, shall keep your hearts and minds through Christ Jesus.

Philippians 4:7

For God hath not given us the spirit of fear; but of power, and of love, and of a sound mind.

II Timothy 1:7

Who hath saved us, and called us with an holy calling, not according to our works, but according to his own purpose and grace, which was given us in Christ Jesus before the world began.

II Timothy 1:9

Because thou hast kept the word of my patience, I also will keep thee from the hour of temptation, which shall come upon all the world, to try them that dwell upon the earth.

Revelation 3:10

For their redeemer is mighty; he shall plead their cause with thee.

Proverbs 23:11

Thus saith the LORD, your redeemer, the Holy One of Israel; For your sake I have sent to Babylon, and have brought down all their nobles, and the Chaldeans, whose cry is in the ships.

Isaiah 43:14

Their Redeemer is strong; the LORD of hosts is his name: he shall throughly plead their cause, that he may give rest to the land, and disquiet the inhabitants of Babylon.

Jeremiah 50:34

The God of my rock; in him will I trust: he is my shield, and the horn of my salvation, my high tower, and my refuge, my saviour; thou savest me from violence.

II Samuel 22:3

My goodness, and my fortress; my high tower, and my deliverer; my shield, and he in whom I trust; who subdueth my people under me.

Psalms 144:2

My help cometh from the LORD, which made heaven and earth.

Psalms 121:2

He will not suffer thy foot to be moved: he that keepeth thee will not slumber.

Psalms 121:3

Behold, he that keepeth Israel shall neither slumber nor sleep.

Psalms 121:4

The LORD is thy keeper: the LORD is thy shade upon thy right hand.

Psalms 121:5

The sun shall not smite thee by day, nor the moon by night.

Psalms 121:6

The LORD shall preserve thee from all evil: he shall preserve thy soul.

Psalms 121:7

The LORD shall preserve thy going out and thy coming in from this time forth, and even for evermore.

Psalms 121:8

And except those days should be shortened, there should no flesh be saved: but for the elect's sake those days shall be shortened.

Matthew 24:22

~ Strength ~

Let the words of my mouth, and the meditation of my heart, be acceptable in thy sight, O LORD, my strength, and my redeemer.

Psalms 19:14

The LORD is my rock, and my fortress, and my deliverer; my God, my strength, in whom I will trust; my buckler, and the horn of my salvation, and my high tower.

Psalms 18:2

I can do all things through Christ which strengtheneth me.

Philippians 4:13

That which we have seen and heard declare we unto you, that ye also may have fellowship with us: and truly our fellowship is with the Father, and with his Son Jesus Christ.

I John 1:3

And he said unto me, My grace is sufficient for thee: for my strength is made perfect in weakness. Most gladly therefore will I rather glory in my infirmities, that the power of Christ may rest upon me.

II Corinthians 12:9

And such trust have we through Christ to Godward.

II Corinthians 3:4

Not that we are sufficient of ourselves to think any thing as of ourselves; but our sufficiency is of God.

II Corinthians 3:5

Notwithstanding the Lord stood with me, and strengthened me; that by me the preaching might be fully known, and that all the Gentiles might hear: and I was delivered out of the mouth of the lion.

II Timothy 4:17

And the Lord shall deliver me from every evil work, and will preserve me unto his heavenly kingdom: to whom be glory for ever and ever. Amen.

II Timothy 4:18

But he answered and said, It is written, Man shall not live by bread alone, but by every word that proceedeth out of the mouth of God.

Matthew 4:4

Abide in me, and I in you. As the branch cannot bear fruit of itself, except it abide in the vine; no more can ye, except ye abide in me.

John 15:4

I am the vine, ye are the branches: He that abideth in me, and I in him, the same bringeth forth much fruit: for without me ye can do nothing.

John 15:5

If a man abide not in me, he is cast forth as a branch, and is withered; and men gather them, and cast them into the fire, and they are burned.

John 15:6

If ye abide in me, and my words abide in you, ye shall ask what ye will, and it shall be done unto you.

John 15:7

But the God of all grace, who hath called us unto his eternal glory by Christ Jesus, after that ye have suffered a while, make you perfect, stablish, strengthen, settle you.

I Peter 5:10

To him be glory and dominion for ever and ever. Amen.

I Peter 5:11

For God hath not given us the spirit of fear; but of power, and of love, and of a sound mind.

II Timothy 1:7

Who hath saved us, and called us with an holy calling, not according to our works, but according to his own purpose and grace, which was given us in Christ Jesus before the world began.

II Timothy 1:9

My soul, wait thou only upon God; for my expectation is from him.

Psalms 62:5

He only is my rock and my salvation: he is my defence; I shall not be moved.

Psalms 62:6

In God is my salvation and my glory: the rock of my strength, and my refuge, is in God.

Psalms 62:7

~ *Truth* ~

Thus saith the LORD the King of Israel, and his redeemer the LORD of hosts; I am the first, and I am the last; and beside me there is no God.

Isaiah 44:6

Thus saith the LORD, thy redeemer, and he that formed thee from the womb, I am the LORD that maketh all things; that stretcheth forth the heavens alone; that spreadeth abroad the earth by myself.;

Isaiah 44:24

I, even I, am the LORD; and beside me there is no saviour.

Isaiah 43:11

Jesus saith unto him, I am the way, the truth, and the life: no man cometh unto the Father, but by me.

John 14:6

But I fear, lest by any means, as the serpent beguiled Eve through his subtilty, so your minds should be corrupted from the simplicity that is in Christ.

II Corinthians 11:3

Sanctify them through thy truth: thy word is truth.

John 17:17

Nevertheless I tell you the truth; It is expedient for you that I go away: for if I go not away, the Comforter will not come unto you; but if I depart, I will send him unto you.

John 16:7

And when he is come, he will reprove the world of sin, and of righteousness, and of judgment.

John 16:8

Of sin, because they believe not on me.

John 16:9

Of righteousness, because I go to my Father, and ye see me no more.

John 16:10

Of judgment, because the prince of this world is judged.

John 16:11

I have yet many things to say unto you, but ye cannot bear them now.

John 16:12

Howbeit when he, the Spirit of truth, is come, he will guide you into all truth: for he shall not speak of himself; but whatsoever he shall hear, that shall he speak: and he will shew you things to come.

John 16:13

He shall glorify me: for he shall receive of mine, and shall shew it unto you.

John 16:14

All things that the Father hath are mine: therefore said I, that he shall take of mine, and shall shew it unto you.

John 16:15

A little while, and ye shall not see me: and again, a little while, and ye shall see me, because I go to the Father.

John 16:16

Hereby know ye the Spirit of God: Every spirit that confesseth that Jesus Christ is come in the flesh is of God.

I John 4:2

God is a Spirit: and they that worship him must worship him in spirit and in truth.

John 4:24

And the Word was made flesh, and dwelt among us, (and we beheld his glory, the glory as of the only begotten of the Father,) full of grace and truth.

John 1:14

For the law was given by Moses, but grace and truth came by Jesus Christ.

John 1:17

And ye shall know the truth, and the truth shall make you free.

John 8:32

The elder unto the elect lady and her children, whom I love in the truth; and not I only, but also all they that have known the truth.

II John 1:1

For the truth's sake, which dwelleth in us, and shall be with us for ever.

II John 1:2

Grace be with you, mercy, and peace, from God the Father, and from the Lord Jesus Christ, the Son of the Father, in truth and love.

II John 1:3

~ *Wisdom* ~

It is the spirit that quickeneth; the flesh profiteth nothing: the words that I speak unto you, they are spirit, and they are life.

John 6:63

For it is not ye that speak, but the Spirit of your Father which speaketh in you.

Matthew 10:20

For the Holy Ghost shall teach you in the same hour what ye ought to say.

Luke 12:12

He that is faithful in that which is least is faithful also in much: and he that is unjust in the least is unjust also in much.

Luke 16:10

If therefore ye have not been faithful in the unrighteous mammon, who will commit to your trust the true riches?

Luke 16:11

And if ye have not been faithful in that which is another man's, who shall give you that which is your own?

Luke 16:12

No servant can serve two masters: for either he will hate the one, and love the other; or else he will hold to the one, and despise the other. Ye cannot serve God and mammon.

Luke 16:13

Settle it therefore in your hearts, not to meditate before what ye shall answer.

Luke 21:14

For I will give you a mouth and wisdom, which all your adversaries shall not be able to gainsay nor resist.

Luke 21:15

The queen of the south shall rise up in the judgment with this generation, and shall condemn it: for she came from the uttermost parts of the earth to hear the wisdom of Solomon; and, behold, a greater than Solomon is here.

Matthew 12:42

And when he was come into his own country, he taught them in their synagogue, insomuch that they were astonished, and said, Whence hath this man this wisdom, and these mighty works?

Matthew 13:54

And Jesus increased in wisdom and stature, and in favour with God and man.

Luke 2:52

But of him are ye in Christ Jesus, who of God is made unto us wisdom, and righteousness, and sanctification, and redemption.

I Corinthians 1:30

To give knowledge of salvation unto his people by the remission of their sins.

Luke 1:77

In that hour Jesus rejoiced in spirit, and said, I thank thee, O Father, Lord of heaven and earth, that thou hast hid these things from the wise and prudent, and hast revealed them unto babes: even so, Father; for so it seemed good in thy sight.

Luke 10:21

Howbeit when he, the Spirit of truth, is come, he will guide you into all truth: for he shall not speak of himself; but whatsoever he shall hear, that shall he speak: and he will shew you things to come.

John 16:13

If any of you lack wisdom, let him ask of God, that giveth to all men liberally, and upbraideth not; and it shall be given him.

James 1:5

God's Promises through...

CHRIST'S PURPOSES

God's Promises through...

CHRIST'S PURPOSES

"For this purpose the Son of God was manifested, that HE might destroy the works of the devil."

I John 3:8

THE PROMISES OF OBTAINING:

~ Answers ~

For every one that asketh receiveth; and he that seeketh findeth; and to him that knocketh it shall be opened.

Matthew 7:8

If ye then, being evil, know how to give good gifts unto your children, how much more shall your Father which is in heaven give good things to them that ask him?

Matthew 7:11

And I say unto you, Ask, and it shall be given you; seek, and ye shall find; knock, and it shall be opened unto you.

Luke 11:9

And I will give him the morning star.

Revelation 2:28

If ye shall ask any thing in my name, I will do it.

John 14:14

And I will pray the Father, and he shall give you another Comforter, that he may abide with you for ever.

John 14:16

Even the Spirit of truth; whom the world cannot receive, because it seeth him not, neither knoweth him: but ye know him; for he dwelleth with you, and shall be in you.

John 14:17

I will not leave you comfortless: I will come to you.

John 14:18

For verily I say unto you, That whosoever shall say unto this mountain, Be thou removed, and be thou cast into the sea; and shall not doubt in his heart, but shall believe that those things which he saith shall come to pass; he shall have whatsoever he saith.

Mark 11:23

Therefore I say unto you, What things soever ye desire, when ye pray, believe that ye receive them, and ye shall have them.

Mark 11:24

And in that day ye shall ask me nothing. Verily, verily, I say unto you, Whatsoever ye shall ask the Father in my name, he will give it you.

John 16:23

And all things, whatsoever ye shall ask in prayer, believing, ye shall receive.

Matthew 21:22

Consider the ravens: for they neither sow nor reap; which neither have storehouse nor barn; and God feedeth them: how much more are ye better than the fowls?

Luke 12:24

But my God shall supply all your need according to his riches in glory by Christ Jesus.

Philippians 4:19

Verily I say unto you, Whatsoever ye shall bind on earth shall be bound in heaven: and whatsoever ye shall loose on earth shall be loosed in heaven.

Matthew 18:18

Again I say unto you, That if two of you shall agree on earth as touching any thing that they shall ask, it shall be done for them of my Father which is in heaven.

Matthew 18:19

Let us therefore come boldly unto the throne of grace, that we may obtain mercy, and find grace to help in time of need.

Hebrews 4:16

Be careful for nothing; but in every thing by prayer and supplication with thanksgiving let your requests be made known unto God.

Philippians 4:6

And the peace of God, which passeth all understanding, shall keep your hearts and minds through Christ Jesus.

Philippians 4:7

And when thou prayest, thou shalt not be as the hypocrites are: for they love to pray standing in the synagogues and in the corners of the streets, that they may be seen of men. Verily I say unto you, They have their reward.

Matthew 6:5

But thou, when thou prayest, enter into thy closet, and when thou hast shut thy door, pray to thy Father which is in secret; and thy Father which seeth in secret shall reward thee openly.

Matthew 6:6

And he spake a parable unto them to this end, that men ought always to pray, and not to faint.

Luke 18:1

And this is the confidence that we have in him, that, if we ask any thing according to his will, he heareth us.

I John 5:14

And if we know that he hear us, whatsoever we ask, we know that we have the petitions that we desired of him.

I John 5:15

Whereby are given unto us exceeding great and precious promises: that by these ye might be partakers of the divine nature, having escaped the corruption that is in the world through lust.

II Peter 1:4

And beside this, giving all diligence, add to your faith virtue; and to virtue knowledge.

II Peter 1:5

And to knowledge temperance; and to temperance patience; and to patience godliness.

II Peter 1:6

And to godliness brotherly kindness; and to brotherly kindness charity.

II Peter 1:7

For if these things be in you, and abound, they make you that ye shall neither be barren nor unfruitful in the knowledge of our Lord Jesus Christ.

II Peter 1:8

For with God nothing shall be impossible.

Luke 1:37

~ Atonement ~

But he was wounded for our transgressions, he was bruised for our iniquities: the chastisement of our peace was upon him; and with his stripes we are healed.

Isaiah 53:5

For if, when we were enemies, we were reconciled to God by the death of his Son, much more, being reconciled, we shall be saved by his life.

Romans 5:10

And not only so, but we also joy in God through our Lord Jesus Christ, by whom we have now received the atonement.

Romans 5:11

And the blood shall be to you for a token upon the houses where ye are: and when I see the blood, I will pass over you, and the plague shall not be upon you to destroy you, when I smite the land of Egypt.

Exodus 12:13

Take heed therefore unto yourselves, and to all the flock, over the which the Holy Ghost hath made you overseers, to feed the church of God, which he hath purchased with his own blood.

Acts 20:28

For he hath made him to be sin for us, who knew no sin; that we might be made the righteousness of God in him.

II Corinthians 5:21

And all that dwell upon the earth shall worship him, whose names are not written in the book of life of the Lamb slain from the foundation of the world.

Revelation 13:8

How much more shall the blood of Christ, who through the eternal Spirit offered himself without spot to God, purge your conscience from dead works to serve the living God?

Hebrews 9:14

And almost all things are by the law purged with blood; and without shedding of blood is no remission.

Hebrews 9:22

Of how much sorer punishment, suppose ye, shall he be thought worthy, who hath trodden under foot the Son of God, and hath counted the blood of the covenant, wherewith he was sanctified, an unholy thing, and hath done despite unto the Spirit of grace?

Hebrews 10:29

Greater love hath no man than this, that a man lay down his life for his friends.

John 15:13

For by grace are ye saved through faith; and that not of yourselves: it is the gift of God:

Ephesians 2:8

But now in Christ Jesus ye who sometimes were far off are made nigh by the blood of Christ.

Ephesians 2:13

And he took bread, and gave thanks, and brake it, and gave unto them, saying, This is my body which is given for you: this do in remembrance of me.

Luke 22:19

And he bearing his cross went forth into a place called the place of a skull, which is called in the Hebrew Golgotha.

John 19:17

But one of the soldiers with a spear pierced his side, and forthwith came there out blood and water.

John 19:34

And he began to teach them, that the Son of man must suffer many things, and be rejected of the elders, and of the chief priests, and scribes, and be killed, and after three days rise again.

Mark 8:31

And he made his grave with the wicked, and with the rich in his death; because he had done no violence, neither was any deceit in his mouth.

Isaiah 53:9

Yet it pleased the LORD to bruise him; he hath put him to grief: when thou shalt make his soul an offering for sin, he shall see his seed, he shall prolong his days, and the pleasure of the LORD shall prosper in his hand.

Isaiah 53:10

He shall see of the travail of his soul, and shall be satisfied: by his knowledge shall my righteous servant justify many; for he shall bear their iniquities.

Isaiah 53:11

Therefore will I divide him a portion with the great, and he shall divide the spoil with the strong; because he hath poured out his soul unto death: and he was numbered with the transgressors; and he bare the sin of many, and made intercession for the transgressors.

Isaiah 53:12

She hath done what she could: she is come aforehand to anoint my body to the burying.

Mark 14:8

Then saith Jesus unto them, All ye shall be offended because of me this night: for it is written, I will smite the shepherd, and the sheep of the flock shall be scattered abroad.

Matthew 26:31

And being found in fashion as a man, he humbled himself, and became obedient unto death, even the death of the cross.

Philippians 2:8

Blotting out the handwriting of ordinances that was against us, which was contrary to us, and took it out of the way, nailing it to his cross.

Colossians 2:14

He that committeth sin is of the devil; for the devil sinneth from the beginning. For this purpose the Son of God was manifested, that he might destroy the works of the devil.

I John 3:8

Who is he that condemneth? It is Christ that died, yea rather, that is risen again, who is even at the right hand of God, who also maketh intercession for us.

Romans 8:34

For I delivered unto you first of all that which I also received, how that Christ died for our sins according to the scriptures.

I Corinthians 15:3

For when we were yet without strength, in due time Christ died for the ungodly.

Romans 5:6

But God commendeth his love toward us, in that, while we were yet sinners, Christ died for us.

Romans 5:8

Likewise also the cup after supper, saying, This cup is the new testament in my blood, which is shed for you.

Luke 22:20

Saying, Father, if thou be willing, remove this cup from me: nevertheless not my will, but thine, be done.

Luke 22:42

Then said Jesus unto Peter, Put up thy sword into the sheath: the cup which my Father hath given me, shall I not drink it?

John 18:11

Verily, verily, I say unto you, Except a corn of wheat fall into the ground and die, it abideth alone: but if it die, it bringeth forth much fruit.

John 12:24

This he said, signifying what death he should die.

John 12:33

That the saying of Jesus might be fulfilled, which he spake, signifying what death he should die.

John 18:32

Jesus, when he had cried again with a loud voice, yielded up the ghost.

Matthew 27:50

For when we were yet without strength, in due time Christ died for the ungodly.

Romans 5:6

For scarcely for a righteous man will one die: yet peradventure for a good man some would even dare to die.

Romans 5:7

Let us therefore follow after the things which make for peace, and things wherewith one may edify another.

Romans 14:19

Who is he that condemneth? It is Christ that died, yea rather, that is risen again, who is even at the right hand of God, who also maketh intercession for us.

Romans 8:34

For the love of Christ constraineth us; because we thus judge, that if one died for all, then were all dead.

II Corinthians 5:14

Now ye are clean through the word which I have spoken unto you.

John 15:3

I gave my back to the smiters, and my cheeks to them that plucked off the hair: I hid not my face from shame and spitting.

Isaiah 50:6

And having spoiled principalities and powers, he made a shew of them openly, triumphing over them in it.

Colossians 2:15

I am he that liveth, and was dead; and, behold, I am alive for evermore, Amen; and have the keys of hell and of death.

Revelation 1:18

Ye are of God, little children, and have overcome them: because greater is he that is in you, than he that is in the world.

I John 4:4

Behold, I give unto you power to tread on serpents and scorpions, and over all the power of the enemy: and nothing shall by any means hurt you.

Luke 10:19

Likewise also the cup after supper, saying, This cup is the new testament in my blood, which is shed for you.

Luke 22:20

For ye are bought with a price: therefore glorify God in your body, and in your spirit, which are God's.

I Corinthians 6:20

For God so loved the world, that he gave his only begotten Son, that whosoever believeth in him should not perish, but have everlasting life.

John 3:16

He shall see of the travail of his soul, and shall be satisfied: by his knowledge shall my righteous servant justify many; for he shall bear their iniquities.

Isaiah 53:11

For this is my blood of the new testament, which is shed for many for the remission of sins.

Matthew 26:28

But God commendeth his love toward us, in that, while we were yet sinners, Christ died for us.

Romans 5:8

Much more then, being now justified by his blood, we shall be saved from wrath through him.

Romans 5:9

For if, when we were enemies, we were reconciled to God by the death of his Son, much more, being reconciled, we shall be saved by his life.

Romans 5:10

Looking unto Jesus the author and finisher of our faith; who for the joy that was set before him endured the cross, despising the shame, and is set down at the right hand of the throne of God.

Hebrews 12:2

In whom we have redemption through his blood, the forgiveness of sins, according to the riches of his grace.

Ephesians 1:7

The eyes of your understanding being enlightened; that ye may know what is the hope of his calling, and what the riches of the glory of his inheritance in the saints.

Ephesians 1:18

And what is the exceeding greatness of his power to us-ward who believe, according to the working of his mighty power.

Ephesians 1:19

Which he wrought in Christ, when he raised him from the dead, and set him at his own right hand in the heavenly places.

Ephesians 1:20

Far above all principality, and power, and might, and dominion, and every name that is named, not only in this world, but also in that which is to come.

Ephesians 1:21

And from Jesus Christ, who is the faithful witness, and the first begotten of the dead, and the prince of the kings of the earth. Unto him that loved us, and washed us from our sins in his own blood.

Revelation 1:5

~ Blessings ~

But ye shall receive power, after that the Holy Ghost is come upon you: and ye shall be witnesses unto me both in Jerusalem, and in all Judaea, and in Samaria, and unto the uttermost part of the earth.

Acts 1:8

Blessed are they which do hunger and thirst after righteousness: for they shall be filled.

Matthew 5:6

And Jesus said unto them, I am the bread of life: he that cometh to me shall never hunger; and he that believeth on me shall never thirst.

John 6:35

But seek ye first the kingdom of God, and his righteousness; and all these things shall be added unto you.

Matthew 6:33

Every good gift and every perfect gift is from above, and cometh down from the Father of lights, with whom is no variableness, neither shadow of turning.

James 1:17

The Lord is not slack concerning his promise, as some men count slackness; but is longsuffering to us-ward, not willing that any should perish, but that all should come to repentance.

II Peter 3:9

And this gospel of the kingdom shall be preached in all the world for a witness unto all nations; and then shall the end come.

Matthew 24:14

And, behold, I send the promise of my Father upon you: but tarry ye in the city of Jerusalem, until ye be endued with power from on high.

Luke 24:49

He will swallow up death in victory; and the Lord GOD will wipe away tears from off all faces; and the rebuke of his people shall he take away from off all the earth: for the LORD hathspoken it.

Isaiah 25:8

There is therefore now no condemnation to them which are in Christ Jesus, who walk not after the flesh, but after the Spirit.

Romans 8:1

For the law of the Spirit of life in Christ Jesus hath made me free from the law of sin and death.

Romans 8:2

For they that are after the flesh do mind the things of the flesh; but they that are after the Spirit the things of the Spirit.

Romans 8:5

For to be carnally minded is death; but to be spiritually minded is life and peace.

Romans 8:6

And the scripture, foreseeing that God would justify the heathen through faith, preached before the gospel unto Abraham, saying, In thee shall all nations be blessed.

Galatians 3:8

Wherefore God also hath highly exalted him, and given him a name which is above every name.

Philippians 2:9

That at the name of Jesus every knee should bow, of things in heaven, and things in earth, and things under the earth.

Philippians 2:10

And that every tongue should confess that Jesus Christ is Lord, to the glory of God the Father.

Philippians 2:11

Wherefore, my beloved, as ye have always obeyed, not as in my presence only, but now much more in my absence, work out your own salvation with fear and trembling.

Philippians 2:12

After this I beheld, and, lo, a great multitude, which no man could number, of all nations, and kindreds, and people, and tongues, stood before the throne, and before the Lamb, clothed with white robes, and palms in their hands.

Revelation 7:9

For unto us a child is born, unto us a son is given: and the government shall be upon his shoulder: and his name shall be called Wonderful, Counsellor, The mighty God, The everlasting Father, The Prince of Peace.

Isaiah 9:6

~ *Comfort* ~

And when the Lord saw her, he had compassion on her, and said unto her, Weep not.

Luke 7:13

So Jesus had compassion on them, and touched their eyes: and immediately their eyes received sight, and they followed him.

Matthew 20:34

The spirit of the Lord GOD is upon me; because the LORD hath anointed me to preach good tidings unto the meek; he hath sent me to bind up the brokenhearted, to proclaim liberty to the captives, and the opening of the prison to them that are bound.

Isaiah 61:1

To proclaim the acceptable year of the LORD, and the day of vengeance of our God; to comfort all that mourn.

Isaiah 61:2

To appoint unto them that mourn in Zion, to give unto them beauty for ashes, the oil of joy for mourning, the garment of praise for the spirit of heaviness; that they might be called trees of righteousness, the planting of the LORD, that he might be glorified.

Isaiah 61:3

But Jesus turned him about, and when he saw her, he said, Daughter, be of good comfort; thy faith hath made thee whole. And the woman was made whole from that hour.

Matthew 9:22

And Jesus stood still, and commanded him to be called. And they call the blind man, saying unto him, Be of good comfort, rise; he calleth thee.

Mark 10:49

And he said unto her, Daughter, be of good comfort: thy faith hath made thee whole; go in peace.

Luke 8:48

Blessed be God, even the Father of our Lord Jesus Christ, the Father of mercies, and the God of all comfort.

II Corinthians 1:3

Who comforteth us in all our tribulation, that we may be able to comfort them which are in any trouble, by the comfort wherewith we ourselves are comforted of God.

II Corinthians 1:4

And he said unto me, My grace is sufficient for thee: for my strength is made perfect in weakness. Most gladly therefore will I rather glory in my infirmities, that the power of Christ may rest upon me.

II Corinthians 12:9

Casting all your care upon him; for he careth for you.

I Peter 5:7

I will not leave you comfortless: I will come to you.

John 14:18

Come unto me, all ye that labour and are heavy laden, and I will give you rest.

Matthew 11:28

Take my yoke upon you, and learn of me; for I am meek and lowly in heart: and ye shall find rest unto your souls.

Matthew 11:29

For my yoke is easy, and my burden is light.

Matthew 11:30

And I will pray the Father, and he shall give you another Comforter, that he may abide with you for ever.

John 14:16

Even the Spirit of truth; whom the world cannot receive, because it seeth him not, neither knoweth him: but ye know him; for he dwelleth with you, and shall be in you.

John 14:17

Peace I leave with you, my peace I give unto you: not as the world giveth, give I unto you. Let not your heart be troubled, neither let it be afraid.

John 14:27

Blessed are the meek: for they shall inherit the earth.

Matthew 5:5

He maketh me to lie down in green pastures: he leadeth me beside the still waters.

Psalms 23:2

For the Lamb which is in the midst of the throne shall feed them, and shall lead them unto living fountains of waters: and God shall wipe away all tears from their eyes.

Revelation 7:17

And Jesus came and touched them, and said, Arise, and be not afraid.

Matthew 17:7

And the peace of God, which passeth all understanding, shall keep your hearts and minds through Christ Jesus.

Philippians 4:7

There remaineth therefore a rest to the people of God.

Hebrews 4:9

Let us labour therefore to enter into that rest, lest any man fall after the same example of unbelief.

Hebrews 4:11

Seeing then that we have a great high priest, that is passed into the heavens, Jesus the Son of God, let us hold fast our profession.

Hebrews 4:14

~ *Deliverance* ~

The spirit of the Lord GOD is upon me; because the LORD hath anointed me to preach good tidings unto the meek; he hath sent me to bind up the brokenhearted, to proclaim liberty to the captives, and the opening of the prison to them that are bound.

Isaiah 61:1

If the Son therefore shall make you free, ye shall be free indeed.

John 8:36

But there shall not an hair of your head perish.

Luke 21:18

And ye shall know the truth, and the truth shall make you free.

John 8:32

And it shall be for a sign and for a witness unto the LORD of hosts in the land of Egypt: for they shall cry unto the LORD because of the oppressors, and he shall send them a saviour, and a great one, and he shall deliver them.

Isaiah 19:20

Notwithstanding the Lord stood with me, and strengthened me; that by me the preaching might be fully known, and that all the Gentiles might hear: and I was delivered out of the mouth of the lion.

II Timothy 4:17

And the Lord shall deliver me from every evil work, and will preserve me unto his heavenly kingdom: to whom be glory for ever and ever. Amen.

II Timothy 4:18

There is therefore now no condemnation to them which are in Christ Jesus, who walk not after the flesh, but after the Spirit.

Romans 8:1

For the law of the Spirit of life in Christ Jesus hath made me free from the law of sin and death.

Romans 8:2

Now the Lord is that Spirit: and where the Spirit of the Lord is, there is liberty.

II Corinthians 3:17

And he that was dead came forth, bound hand and foot with graveclothes: and his face was bound about with a napkin. Jesus saith unto them, Loose him, and let him go.

John 11:44

For he said unto him, Come out of the man, thou unclean spirit.

Mark 5:8

And they come to Jesus, and see him that was possessed with the devil, and had the legion, sitting, and clothed, and in his right mind: and they were afraid.

Mark 5:15

The LORD is my rock, and my fortress, and my deliverer; my God, my strength, in whom I will trust; my buckler, and the horn of my salvation, and my high tower.

Psalms 18:2

Notwithstanding the Lord stood with me, and strengthened me; that by me the preaching might be fully known, and that all the Gentiles might hear: and I was delivered out of the mouth of the lion.

II Timothy 4:17

And the Lord shall deliver me from every evil work, and will preserve me unto his heavenly kingdom: to whom be glory for ever and ever. Amen.

II Timothy 4:18

Are not two sparrows sold for a farthing? and one of them shall not fall on the ground without your Father.

Matthew 10:29

But the very hairs of your head are all numbered.

Matthew 10:30

Fear ye not therefore, ye are of more value than many sparrows.

Matthew 10:31

For he is our peace, who hath made both one, and hath broken down the middle wall of partition between us.

Ephesians 2:14

~ *Forgiveness* ~

In a little wrath I hid my face from thee for a moment; but with everlasting kindness will I have mercy on thee, saith the LORD thy Redeemer.

Isaiah 54:8

Him hath God exalted with his right hand to be a Prince and a Saviour, for to give repentance to Israel, and forgiveness of sins.

Acts 5:31

If we confess our sins, he is faithful and just to forgive us our sins, and to cleanse us from all unrighteousness.

I John 1:9

For by grace are ye saved through faith; and that not of yourselves: it is the gift of God.

Ephesians 2:8

In whom we have redemption through his blood, the forgiveness of sins, according to the riches of his grace;

Ephesians 1:7

Jesus saith unto him, I say not unto thee, Until seven times: but, Until seventy times seven.

Matthew 18:22

Then said Jesus, Father, forgive them; for they know not what they do. And they parted his raiment, and cast lots.

Luke 23:34

And when ye stand praying, forgive, if ye have ought against any: that your Father also which is in heaven may forgive you your trespasses.

Mark 11:25

And ye know that he was manifested to take away our sins; and in him is no sin.

I John 3:5

Whosoever abideth in him sinneth not: whosoever sinneth hath not seen him, neither known him.

I John 3:6

To wit, that God was in Christ, reconciling the world unto himself, not imputing their trespasses unto them; and hath committed unto us the word of reconciliation.

II Corinthians 5:19

And you, being dead in your sins and the uncircumcision of your flesh, hath he quickened together with him, having forgiven you all trespasses.

Colossians 2:13

I have blotted out, as a thick cloud, thy transgressions, and, as a cloud, thy sins: return unto me; for I have redeemed thee.

Isaiah 44:22

~ *Glorification* ~

I have glorified thee on the earth: I have finished the work which thou gavest me to do.

John 17:4

And now, O Father, glorify thou me with thine own self with the glory which I had with thee before the world was.

John 17:5

That at the name of Jesus every knee should bow, of things in heaven, and things in earth, and things under the earth.

Philippians 2:10

And that every tongue should confess that Jesus Christ is Lord, to the glory of God the Father.

Philippians 2:11

Jesus saith unto them, My meat is to do the will of him that sent me, and to finish his work.

John 4:34

I can of mine own self do nothing: as I hear, I judge: and my judgment is just; because I seek not mine own will, but the will of the Father which hath sent me.

John 5:30

Yet ye have not known him; but I know him: and if I should say, I know him not, I shall be a liar like unto you: but I know him, and keep his saying.

John 8:55

He that speaketh of himself seeketh his own glory: but he that seeketh his glory that sent him, the same is true, and no unrighteousness is in him.

John 7:18

Jesus answered, I have not a devil; but I honour my Father, and ye do dishonour me.

John 8:49

And I seek not mine own glory: there is one that seeketh and judgeth.

John 8:50

Therefore, when he was gone out, Jesus said, Now is the Son of man glorified, and God is glorified in him.

John 13:31

If God be glorified in him, God shall also glorify him in himself, and shall straightway glorify him.

John 13:32

But that the world may know that I love the Father; and as the Father gave me commandment, even so I do. Arise, let us go hence.

John 14:31

These words spake Jesus, and lifted up his eyes to heaven, and said, Father, the hour is come; glorify thy Son, that thy Son also may glorify thee.

John 17:1

And he said, Abba, Father, all things are possible unto thee; take away this cup from me: nevertheless not what I will, but what thou wilt.

Mark 14:36

Who being the brightness of his glory, and the express image of his person, and upholding all things by the word of his power, when he had by himself purged our sins, sat down on the right hand of the Majesty on high.

Hebrews 1:3

Being made so much better than the angels, as he hath by inheritance obtained a more excellent name than they.

Hebrews 1:4

For unto which of the angels said he at any time, Thou art my Son, this day have I begotten thee? And again, I will be to him a Father, and he shall be to me a Son?

Hebrews 1:5

And again, when he bringeth in the firstbegotten into the world, he saith, And let all the angels of God worship him.

Hebrews 1:6

But when the multitudes saw it, they marvelled, and glorified God, which had given such power unto men.

Matthew 9:8

Father, glorify thy name. Then came there a voice from heaven, saying, I have both glorified it, and will glorify it again.

John 12:28

This spake he, signifying by what death he should glorify God. And when he had spoken this, he saith unto him, Follow me.

John 21:19

~ *Grace* ~

And the Word was made flesh, and dwelt among us, (and we beheld his glory, the glory as of the only begotten of the Father,) full of grace and truth.

John 1:14

And of his fulness have all we received, and grace for grace.

John 1:16

For the law was given by Moses, but grace and truth came by Jesus Christ.

John 1:17

But we believe that through the grace of the Lord Jesus Christ we shall be saved, even as they.

Acts 15:11

Being justified freely by his grace through the redemption that is in Christ Jesus:

Romans 3:24

But not as the offence, so also is the free gift. For if through the offence of one many be dead, much more the grace of God, and the gift by grace, which is by one man, Jesus Christ, hath abounded unto many.

Romans 5:15

And not as it was by one that sinned, so is the gift: for the judgment was by one to condemnation, but the free gift is of many offences unto justification.

Romans 5:16

For if by one man's offence death reigned by one; much more they which receive abundance of grace and of the gift of righteousness shall reign in life by one, Jesus Christ.)

Romans 5:17

And he said unto me, My grace is sufficient for thee: for my strength is made perfect in weakness. Most gladly therefore will I rather glory in my infirmities, that the power of Christ may rest upon me.

II Corinthians 12:9

In whom we have redemption through his blood, the forgiveness of sins, according to the riches of his grace.

Ephesians 1:7

Having abolished in his flesh the enmity, even the law of commandments contained in ordinances; for to make in himself of twain one new man, so making peace.

Ephesians 2:15

Blotting out the handwriting of ordinances that was against us, which was contrary to us, and took it out of the way, nailing it to his cross.

Colossians 2:14

Then said Jesus, Father, forgive them; for they know not what they do. And they parted his raiment, and cast lots.

Luke 23:34

Teaching them to observe all things whatsoever I have commanded you: and, lo, I am with you alway, even unto the end of the world. Amen.

Matthew 28:20

And Jesus, moved with compassion, put forth his hand, and touched him, and saith unto him, I will; be thou clean.

Mark 1:41

When Jesus heard it, he saith unto them, They that are whole have no need of the physician, but they that are sick: I came not to call the righteous, but sinners to repentance.

Mark 2:17

And Jesus, when he came out, saw much people, and was moved with compassion toward them, because they were as sheep not having a shepherd: and he began to teach them many things.

Mark 6:34

And when he heard that it was Jesus of Nazareth, he began to cry out, and say, Jesus, thou son of David, have mercy on me.

Mark 10:47

And many charged him that he should hold his peace: but he cried the more a great deal, Thou son of David, have mercy on me.

Mark 10:48

And Jesus stood still, and commanded him to be called. And they call the blind man, saying unto him, Be of good comfort, rise; he calleth thee.

Mark 10:49

And the child grew, and waxed strong in spirit, filled with wisdom: and the grace of God was upon him.

Luke 2:40

~ *Guidance* ~

...Give ear, O Shepherd of Israel, thou that leadest Joseph like a flock; thou that dwellest between the cherubims, shine forth.

Psalms 80:1

He that believeth on me, as the scripture hath said, out of his belly shall flow rivers of living water.

John 7:38

Thus saith the LORD, thy Redeemer, the Holy One of Israel; I am the LORD thy God which teacheth thee to profit, which leadeth thee by the way that thou shouldest go.

Isaiah 48:17

Beware of false prophets, which come to you in sheep's clothing, but inwardly they are ravening wolves.

Matthew 7:15

Ye shall know them by their fruits. Do men gather grapes of thorns, or figs of thistles?

Matthew 7:16

Even so every good tree bringeth forth good fruit; but a corrupt tree bringeth forth evil fruit.

Matthew 7:17

And he said unto them, Take heed, and beware of covetousness: for a man's life consisteth not in the abundance of the things which he possesseth.

Luke 12:15

Wherefore if thy hand or thy foot offend thee, cut them off, and cast them from thee: it is better for thee to enter into life halt or maimed, rather than having two hands or two feet to be cast into everlasting fire.

Matthew 18:8

And if thine eye offend thee, pluck it out, and cast it from thee: it is better for thee to enter into life with one eye, rather than having two eyes to be cast into hell fire.

Matthew 18:9

Howbeit when he, the Spirit of truth, is come, he will guide you into all truth: for he shall not speak of himself; but whatsoever he shall hear, that shall he speak: and he will shew you things to come.

John 16:13

If any of you lack wisdom, let him ask of God, that giveth to all men liberally, and upbraideth not; and it shall be given him.

James 1:5

For the Son of man is come to save that which was lost.

Matthew 18:11

Behold, I send you forth as sheep in the midst of wolves: be ye therefore wise as serpents, and harmless as doves.

Matthew 10:16

And he said unto them, Take heed, and beware of covetousness: for a man's life consisteth not in the abundance of the things which he possesseth.

Luke 12:15

But seek ye first the kingdom of God, and his righteousness; and all these things shall be added unto you.

Matthew 6:33

Take therefore no thought for the morrow: for the morrow shall take thought for the things of itself. Sufficient unto the day is the evil thereof.

Matthew 6:34

Settle it therefore in your hearts, not to meditate before what ye shall answer.

Luke 21:14

For I will give you a mouth and wisdom, which all your adversaries shall not be able to gainsay nor resist.

Luke 21:15

For unto us a child is born, unto us a son is given: and the government shall be upon his shoulder: and his name shall be called Wonderful, Counsellor, The mighty God, The everlasting Father, The Prince of Peace.

Isaiah 9:6

~ *Headship* ~

But now hath God set the members every one of them in the body, as it hath pleased him.

I Corinthians 12:18

And he is the head of the body, the church: who is the beginning, the firstborn from the dead; that in all things he might have the preeminence.

Colossians 1:18

There is neither Jew nor Greek, there is neither bond nor free, there is neither male nor female: for ye are all one in Christ Jesus.

Galatians 3:28

For where two or three are gathered together in my name, there am I in the midst of them.

Matthew 18:20

For ye are bought with a price: therefore glorify God in your body, and in your spirit, which are God's.

I Corinthians 6:20

He shall glorify me: for he shall receive of mine, and shall shew it unto you.

John 16:14

All things that the Father hath are mine: therefore said I, that he shall take of mine, and shall shew it unto you.

John 16:15

A little while, and ye shall not see me: and again, a little while, and ye shall see me, because I go to the Father.

John 16:16

Then said some of his disciples among themselves, What is this that he saith unto us, A little while, and ye shall not see me: and again, a little while, and ye shall see me: and, Because I go to the Father?

John 16:17

Howbeit the most High dwelleth not in temples made with hands; as saith the prophet.

Acts 7:48

But he that entereth in by the door is the shepherd of the sheep.

John 10:2

To him the porter openeth; and the sheep hear his voice: and he calleth his own sheep by name, and leadeth them out.

John 10:3

And when he putteth forth his own sheep, he goeth before them, and the sheep follow him: for they know his voice.

John 10:4

And a stranger will they not follow, but will flee from him: for they know not the voice of strangers.

John 10:5

This parable spake Jesus unto them: but they understood not what things they were which he spake unto them.

John 10:6

Then said Jesus unto them again, Verily, verily, I say unto you, I am the door of the sheep

John 10:7 .

All that ever came before me are thieves and robbers: but the sheep did not hear them.

John 10:8

I am the door: by me if any man enter in, he shall be saved, and shall go in and out, and find pasture.

John 10:9

The thief cometh not, but for to steal, and to kill, and to destroy: I am come that they might have life, and that they might have it more abundantly.

John 10:10

I am the good shepherd: the good shepherd giveth his life for the sheep.

John 10:11

I am the good shepherd, and know my sheep, and am known of mine.

John 10:14

As the Father knoweth me, even so know I the Father: and I lay down my life for the sheep.

John 10:15

And other sheep I have, which are not of this fold: them also I must bring, and they shall hear my voice; and there shall be one fold, and one shepherd.

John 10:16

Therefore doth my Father love me, because I lay down my life, that I might take it again.

John 10:17

My sheep hear my voice, and I know them, and they follow me:

John 10:27

And I give unto them eternal life; and they shall never perish, neither shall any man pluck them out of my hand.

John 10:28

John answered, saying unto them all, I indeed baptize you with water; but one mightier than I cometh, the latchet of whose shoes I am not worthy to unloose: he shall baptize you with the Holy Ghost and with fire.

Luke 3:16

Whose fan is in his hand, and he will throughly purge his floor, and will gather the wheat into his garner; but the chaff he will burn with fire unquenchable.

Luke 3:17

And ye are complete in him, which is the head of all principality and power.

Colossians 2:10

Now therefore ye are no more strangers and foreigners, but fellowcitizens with the saints, and of the household of God.

Ephesians 2:19

And are built upon the foundation of the apostles and prophets, Jesus Christ himself being the chief corner stone.

Ephesians 2:20

In whom all the building fitly framed together groweth unto an holy temple in the Lord.

Ephesians 2:21

In whom ye also are builded together for an habitation of God through the Spirit.

Ephesians 2:22

God is faithful, by whom ye were called unto the fellowship of his Son Jesus Christ our Lord.

I Corinthians 1:19

Now I beseech you, brethren, by the name of our Lord Jesus Christ, that ye all speak the same thing, and that there be no divisions among you; but that ye be perfectly joined together in the same mind and in the same judgment.

I Corinthians 1:10

Ye call me Master and Lord: and ye say well; for so I am.

John 13:13

If I then, your Lord and Master, have washed your feet; ye also ought to wash one another's feet.

John 13:14

For I have given you an example, that ye should do as I have done to you.

John 13:15

Verily, verily, I say unto you, The servant is not greater than his lord; neither he that is sent greater than he that sent him.

John 13:16

If ye know these things, happy are ye if ye do them.

John 13:17

Neither pray I for these alone, but for them also which shall believe on me through their word.

John 17:20

That they all may be one; as thou, Father, art in me, and I in thee, that they also may be one in us: that the world may believe that thou hast sent me.

John 17:21

And the glory which thou gavest me I have given them; that they may be one, even as we are one.

John 17:22

I in them, and thou in me, that they may be made perfect in one; and that the world may know that thou hast sent me, and hast loved them, as thou hast loved me.

John 17:23

~ *Healing* ~

So Jesus had compassion on them, and touched their eyes: and immediately their eyes received sight, and they followed him.

Matthew 20:34

And he said unto him, Arise, go thy way: thy faith hath made thee whole.

Luke 17:19

Then Jesus answered and said unto her, O woman, great is thy faith: be it unto thee even as thou wilt. And her daughter was made whole from that very hour.

Matthew 15:28

But he was wounded for our transgressions, he was bruised for our iniquities: the chastisement of our peace was upon him; and with his stripes we are healed.

Isaiah 53:5

And they brought him unto him: and when he saw him, straightway the spirit tare him; and he fell on the ground, and wallowed foaming.

Mark 9:20

And he asked his father, How long is it ago since this came unto him? And he said, Of a child.

Mark 9:21

And ofttimes it hath cast him into the fire, and into the waters, to destroy him: but if thou canst do any thing, have compassion on us, and help us.

Mark 9:22

And ought not this woman, being a daughter of Abraham, whom Satan hath bound, lo, these eighteen years, be loosed from this bond on the sabbath day?

Luke 13:16

But that ye may know that the Son of man hath power upon earth to forgive sins, (he said unto the sick of the palsy,) I say unto thee, Arise, and take up thy couch, and go into thine house.

Luke 5:24

And Jesus said unto the centurion, Go thy way; and as thou hast believed, so be it done unto thee. And his servant was healed in the selfsame hour.

Matthew 8:13

And into whatsoever city ye enter, and they receive you, eat such things as are set before you:

Luke 10:8

And Jesus saith unto him, I will come and heal him.

Matthew 8:7

For whether is easier, to say, Thy sins be forgiven thee; or to say, Arise, and walk?

Matthew 9:5

~ *Justice* ~

I can of mine own self do nothing: as I hear, I judge: and my judgment is just; because I seek not mine own will, but the will of the Father which hath sent me.

John 5:30

Grudge not one against another, brethren, lest ye be condemned: behold, the judge standeth before the door.

James 5:9

I charge thee therefore before God, and the Lord Jesus Christ, who shall judge the quick and the dead at his appearing and his kingdom.

II Timothy 4:1

Henceforth there is laid up for me a crown of righteousness, which the Lord, the righteous judge, shall give me at that day: and not to me only, but unto all them also that love his appearing.

II Timothy 4:8

But why dost thou judge thy brother? or why dost thou set at nought thy brother? for we shall all stand before the judgment seat of Christ.

Romans 14:10

In the day when God shall judge the secrets of men by Jesus Christ according to my gospel.

Romans 2:16

When the Son of man shall come in his glory, and all the holy angels with him, then shall he sit upon the throne of his glory.

Matthew 25:31

And before him shall be gathered all nations: and he shall separate them one from another, as a shepherd divideth his sheep from the goats.

Matthew 25:32

And he shall set the sheep on his right hand, but the goats on the left.

Matthew 25:33

Then shall the King say unto them on his right hand, Come, ye blessed of my Father, inherit the kingdom prepared for you from the foundation of the world.

Matthew 25:34

Behold, the days come, saith the LORD, that I will raise unto David a righteous Branch, and a King shall reign and prosper, and shall execute judgment and justice in the earth.

Jeremiah 23:5

And shall make him of quick understanding in the fear of the LORD: and he shall not judge after the sight of his eyes, neither reprove after the hearing of his ears.

Isaiah 11:3

But with righteousness shall he judge the poor, and reprove with equity for the meek of the earth: and he shall smite the earth with the rod of his mouth, and with the breath of his lips shall he slay the wicked.

Isaiah 11:4

And he commanded us to preach unto the people, and to testify that it is he which was ordained of God to be the Judge of quick and dead.

Acts 10:42

And I saw heaven opened, and behold a white horse; and he that sat upon him was called Faithful and True, and in righteousness he doth judge and make war.

Revelation 19:11

And yet if I judge, my judgment is true: for I am not alone, but I and the Father that sent me.

John 8:16 .

Therefore judge nothing before the time, until the Lord come, who both will bring to light the hidden things of darkness, and will make manifest the counsels of the hearts: and then shall every man have praise of God.

I Corinthians 4:5

But, O LORD of hosts, that judgest righteously, that triest the reins and the heart, let me see thy vengeance on them: for unto thee have I revealed my cause.

Jeremiah 11:20

Who, when he was reviled, reviled not again; when he suffered, he threatened not; but committed himself to him that judgeth righteously.

I Peter 2:23

~ *Light* ~

Then spake Jesus again unto them, saying, I am the light of the world: he that followeth me shall not walk in darkness, but shall have the light of life.

John 8:12

Then Jesus said unto them, Yet a little while is the light with you. Walk while ye have the light, lest darkness come upon you: for he that walketh in darkness knoweth not whither he goeth.

John 12:35

While ye have light, believe in the light, that ye may be the children of light. These things spake Jesus, and departed, and did hide himself from them.

John 12:36

I am come a light into the world, that whosoever believeth on me should not abide in darkness.

John 12:46

And the city had no need of the sun, neither of the moon, to shine in it: for the glory of God did lighten it, and the Lamb is the light thereof.

Revelation 21:23

I Jesus have sent mine angel to testify unto you these things in the churches. I am the root and the offspring of David, and the bright and morning star.

Revelation 22:16

The people which sat in darkness saw great light; and to them which sat in the region and shadow of death light is sprung up.

Matthew 4:16

And was transfigured before them: and his face did shine as the sun, and his raiment was white as the light.

Matthew 17:2

To give light to them that sit in darkness and in the shadow of death, to guide our feet into the way of peace.

Luke 1:79

A light to lighten the Gentiles, and the glory of thy people Israel.

Luke 2:32

In him was life; and the life was the light of men.
John 1:4

And the light shineth in darkness; and the darkness comprehended it not.

John 1:5

And this is the condemnation, that light is come into the world, and men loved darkness rather than light, because their deeds were evil.

John 3:19

As long as I am in the world, I am the light of the world.

John 9:5

Wherefore he saith, Awake thou that sleepest, and arise from the dead, and Christ shall give thee light.

Ephesians 5:14

But is now made manifest by the appearing of our Saviour Jesus Christ, who hath abolished death, and hath brought life and immortality to light through the gospel.

II Timothy 1:10

Who being the brightness of his glory, and the express image of his person, and upholding all things by the word of his power, when he had by himself purged our sins, sat down on the right hand of the Majesty on high.

Hebrews 1:3

~ *Love* ~

Let your conversation be without covetousness; and be content with such things as ye have: for he hath said, I will never leave thee, nor forsake thee.

Hebrews 13:5

If ye keep my commandments, ye shall abide in my love; even as I have kept my Father's commandments, and abide in his love.

John 15:10

These things have I spoken unto you, that my joy might remain in you, and that your joy might be full.

John 15:11

This is my commandment, That ye love one another, as I have loved you.

John 15:12

Herein is love, not that we loved God, but that he loved us, and sent his Son to be the propitiation for our sins.

I John 4:10

But after that the kindness and love of God our Saviour toward man appeared.

Titus 3:4

Now our Lord Jesus Christ himself, and God, even our Father, which hath loved us, and hath given us everlasting consolation and good hope through grace.

II Thessalonians 2:16

Who shall separate us from the love of Christ? shall tribulation, or distress, or persecution, or famine, or nakedness, or peril, or sword?

Romans 8:35

As it is written, For thy sake we are killed all the day long; we are accounted as sheep for the slaughter.

Romans 8:36

Nay, in all these things we are more than conquerors through him that loved us.

Romans 8:37

For I am persuaded, that neither death, nor life, nor angels, nor principalities, nor powers, nor things present, nor things to come.

Romans 8:38

As the Father hath loved me, so have I loved you: continue ye in my love.

John 15:9

This is my commandment, That ye love one another, as I have loved you.

John 15:12

Greater love hath no man than this, that a man lay down his life for his friends.

John 15:13

Ye are my friends, if ye do whatsoever I command you.

John 15:14

And the second is like unto it, Thou shalt love thy neighbour as thyself.

Matthew 22:39

A new commandment I give unto you, That ye love one another; as I have loved you, that ye also love one another.

John 13:34

And I have declared unto them thy name, and will declare it: that the love wherewith thou hast loved me may be in them, and I in them.

John 17:26

But God commendeth his love toward us, in that, while we were yet sinners, Christ died for us.

Romans 5:8

And to know the love of Christ, which passeth knowledge, that ye might be filled with all the fulness of God.

Ephesians 3:19

And walk in love, as Christ also hath loved us, and hath given himself for us an offering and a sacrifice to God for a sweetsmelling savour.

Ephesians 5:2

Hold fast the form of sound words, which thou hast heard of me, in faith and love which is in Christ Jesus.

II Timothy 1:13

For in Jesus Christ neither circumcision availeth any thing, nor uncircumcision; but faith which worketh by love.

Galatians 5:6

As many as I love, I rebuke and chasten: be zealous therefore, and repent.

Revelation 3:19

~ *Mediator* ~

Jesus saith unto him, I am the way, the truth, and the life: no man cometh unto the Father, but by me.

John 14:6

Seeing then that we have a great high priest, that is passed into the heavens, Jesus the Son of God, let us hold fast our profession.

Hebrews 4:14

For Christ is not entered into the holy places made with hands, which are the figures of the true; but into heaven itself, now to appear in the presence of God for us.

Hebrews 9:24

And he saw that there was no man, and wondered that there was no intercessor: therefore his arm brought salvation unto him; and his righteousness, it sustained him.

Isaiah 59:16

For he put on righteousness as a breastplate, and an helmet of salvation upon his head; and he put on the garments of vengeance for clothing, and was clad with zeal as a cloak.

Isaiah 59:17

Wherefore then serveth the law? It was added because of transgressions, till the seed should come to whom the promise was made; and it was ordained by angels in the hand of a mediator.

Galatians 3:19

Now a mediator is not a mediator of one, but God is one.

Galatians 3:20

But now hath he obtained a more excellent ministry, by how much also he is the mediator of a better covenant, which was established upon better promises.

Hebrews 8:6

And for this cause he is the mediator of the new testament, that by means of death, for the redemption of the transgressions that were under the first testament, they which are called might receive the promise of eternal inheritance.

Hebrews 9:15

And to Jesus the mediator of the new covenant, and to the blood of sprinkling, that speaketh better things than that of Abel.

Hebrews 12:24

Being justified freely by his grace through the redemption that is in Christ Jesus.

Romans 3:24

Whom God hath set forth to be a propitiation through faith in his blood, to declare his righteousness for the remission of sins that are past, through the forbearance of God.

Romans 3:25

To declare, I say, at this time his righteousness: that he might be just, and the justifier of him which believeth in Jesus.

Romans 3:26

At that day ye shall ask in my name: and I say not unto you, that I will pray the Father for you.

John 16:26

For the Father himself loveth you, because ye have loved me, and have believed that I came out from God.

John 16:27

And the Lord said, Simon, Simon, behold, Satan hath desired to have you, that he may sift you as wheat.

Luke 22:31

But I have prayed for thee, that thy faith fail not: and when thou art converted, strengthen thy brethren.

Luke 22:32

Then said Jesus, Father, forgive them; for they know not what they do. And they parted his raiment, and cast lots.

Luke 23:34

For he is our peace, who hath made both one, and hath broken down the middle wall of partition between us.

Ephesians 2:14

Now of the things which we have spoken this is the sum: We have such an high priest, who is set on the right hand of the throne of the Majesty in the heavens.

Hebrews 8:1

For then must he often have suffered since the foundation of the world: but now once in the end of the world hath he appeared to put away sin by the sacrifice of himself.

Hebrews 9:26

~ *Overcoming* ~

Knowing this, that our old man is crucified with him, that the body of sin might be destroyed, that henceforth we should not serve sin.

Romans 6:6

For we have not an high priest which cannot be touched with the feeling of our infirmities; but was in all points tempted like as we are, yet without sin.

Hebrews 4:15

For what the law could not do, in that it was weak through the flesh, God sending his own Son in the likeness of sinful flesh, and for sin, condemned sin in the flesh.

Romans 8:3

That the righteousness of the law might be fulfilled in us, who walk not after the flesh, but after the Spirit.

Romans 8:4

For they that are after the flesh do mind the things of the flesh; but they that are after the Spirit the things of the Spirit.

Romans 8:5

For to be carnally minded is death; but to be spiritually minded is life and peace.

Romans 8:6

Because the carnal mind is enmity against God: for it is not subject to the law of God, neither indeed can be.

Romans 8:7

So then they that are in the flesh cannot please God.

Romans 8:8

But ye are not in the flesh, but in the Spirit, if so be that the Spirit of God dwell in you. Now if any man have not the Spirit of Christ, he is none of his.

Romans 8:9

And if Christ be in you, the body is dead because of sin; but the Spirit is life because of righteousness.

Romans 8:10

But if the Spirit of him that raised up Jesus from the dead dwell in you, he that raised up Christ from the dead shall also quicken your mortal bodies by his Spirit that dwelleth in you.

Romans 8:11

Therefore, brethren, we are debtors, not to the flesh, to live after the flesh.

Romans 8:12

Now the works of the flesh are manifest, which are these; Adultery, fornication, uncleanness, lasciviousness,

Galatians 5:19

Idolatry, witchcraft, hatred, variance, emulations, wrath, strife, seditions, heresies,

Galatians 5:20

Envyings, murders, drunkenness, revellings, and such like: of the which I tell you before, as I have also told you in time past, that they which do such things shall not inherit the kingdom of God.

Galatians 5:21

But the fruit of the Spirit is love, joy, peace, long-suffering, gentleness, goodness, faith,

Galatians 5:22

Meekness, temperance: against such there is no law.

Galatians 5:23

And they that are Christ's have crucified the flesh with the affections and lusts.

Galatians 5:24

For Christ also hath once suffered for sins, the just for the unjust, that he might bring us to God, being put to death in the flesh, but quickened by the Spirit.

I Peter 3:18

Forasmuch then as Christ hath suffered for us in the flesh, arm yourselves likewise with the same mind: for he that hath suffered in the flesh hath ceased from sin.

I Peter 4:1

That he no longer should live the rest of his time in the flesh to the lusts of men, but to the will of God.

I Peter 4:2

Having abolished in his flesh the enmity, even the law of commandments contained in ordinances; for to make in himself of twain one new man, so making peace.

Ephesians 2:15

Blotting out the handwriting of ordinances that was against us, which was contrary to us, and took it out of the way, nailing it to his cross.

Colossians 2:14

Wherefore if ye be dead with Christ from the rudiments of the world, why, as though living in the world, are ye subject to ordinances.

Colossians 2:20

For he hath made him to be sin for us, who knew no sin; that we might be made the righteousness of God in him.

II Corinthians 5:21

For we have not an high priest which cannot be touched with the feeling of our infirmities; but was in all points tempted like as we are, yet without sin.

Hebrews 4:15

These things I have spoken unto you, that in me ye might have peace. In the world ye shall have tribulation: but be of good cheer; I have overcome the world.

John 16:33

Ye are of God, little children, and have overcome them: because greater is he that is in you, than he that is in the world.

I John 4:4

These things I have spoken unto you, that in me ye might have peace. In the world ye shall have tribulation: but be of good cheer; I have overcome the world.

John 16:33

Who is he that overcometh the world, but he that believeth that Jesus is the Son of God?

I John 5:5

~ *Prophecy* ~

For he taught his disciples, and said unto them, The Son of man is delivered into the hands of men, and they shall kill him; and after that he is killed, he shall rise the third day.

Mark 9:31

Many will say to me in that day, Lord, Lord, have we not prophesied in thy name? and in thy name have cast out devils? and in thy name done many wonderful works?

Matthew 7:22

When Jesus understood it, he said unto them, Why trouble ye the woman? for she hath wrought a good work upon me.

Matthew 26:10

For ye have the poor always with you; but me ye have not always.

Matthew 26:11

For in that she hath poured this ointment on my body, she did it for my burial.

Matthew 26:12

And, being assembled together with them, commanded them that they should not depart from Jerusalem, but wait for the promise of the Father, which, saith he, ye have heard of me.

Acts 1:4

For John truly baptized with water; but ye shall be baptized with the Holy Ghost not many days hence.

Acts 1:5

O Jerusalem, Jerusalem, thou that killest the prophets, and stonest them which are sent unto thee, how often would I have gathered thy children together, even as a hen gathereth her chickens under her wings, and ye would not!

Matthew 23:37

Behold, your house is left unto you desolate.

Matthew 23:38

But Jesus turning unto them said, Daughters of Jerusalem, weep not for me, but weep for yourselves, and for your children.

Luke 23:28

For, behold, the days are coming, in the which they shall say, Blessed are the barren, and the wombs that never bare, and the paps which never gave suck.

Luke 23:29

Then shall they begin to say to the mountains, Fall on us; and to the hills, Cover us.

Luke 23:30

The men of Nineveh shall rise in judgment with this generation, and shall condemn it: because they repented at the preaching of Jonas; and, behold, a greater than Jonas is here.

Matthew 12:41

And Jesus answered and said unto them, Take heed that no man deceive you.

Matthew 24:4

For many shall come in my name, saying, I am Christ; and shall deceive many.

Matthew 24:5

And ye shall hear of wars and rumours of wars: see that ye be not troubled: for all these things must come to pass, but the end is not yet.

Matthew 24:6

For nation shall rise against nation, and kingdom against kingdom: and there shall be famines, and pestilences, and earthquakes, in divers places.

Matthew 24:7

All these are the beginning of sorrows.

Matthew 24:8

Then shall they deliver you up to be afflicted, and shall kill you: and ye shall be hated of all nations for my name's sake.

Matthew 24:9

And then shall many be offended, and shall betray one another, and shall hate one another.

Matthew 24:10

And many false prophets shall rise, and shall deceive many.

Matthew 24:11

And because iniquity shall abound, the love of many shall wax cold.

Matthew 24:12

But he that shall endure unto the end, the same shall be saved.

Matthew 24:13

And this gospel of the kingdom shall be preached in all the world for a witness unto all nations; and then shall the end come.

Matthew 24:14

And when he was demanded of the Pharisees, when the kingdom of God should come, he answered them and said, The kingdom of God cometh not with observation.

Luke 17:20

Neither shall they say, Lo here! or, lo there! for, behold, the kingdom of God is within you.

Luke 17:21

And he said unto the disciples, The days will come, when ye shall desire to see one of the days of the Son of man, and ye shall not see it.

Luke 17:22

And then shall appear the sign of the Son of man in heaven: and then shall all the tribes of the earth mourn, and they shall see the Son of man coming in the clouds of heaven with power and great glory.

Matthew 24:30

And now I have told you before it come to pass, that, when it is come to pass, ye might believe.

John 14:29

And this is the will of him that sent me, that every one which seeth the Son, and believeth on him, may have everlasting life: and I will raise him up at the last day.

John 6:40

Then shall two be in the field; the one shall be taken, and the other left.

Matthew 24:40

Watch therefore: for ye know not what hour your Lord doth come.

Matthew 24:42

Therefore be ye also ready: for in such an hour as ye think not the Son of man cometh.

Matthew 24:44

But, beloved, remember ye the words which were spoken before of the apostles of our Lord Jesus Christ.

Jude 1:17

How that they told you there should be mockers in the last time, who should walk after their own ungodly lusts.

Jude 1:18

These be they who separate themselves, sensual, having not the Spirit.

Jude 1:19

But ye, beloved, building up yourselves on your most holy faith, praying in the Holy Ghost.

Jude 1:20

Keep yourselves in the love of God, looking for the mercy of our Lord Jesus Christ unto eternal life.

Jude 1:21

~ *Restoration* ~

And they that shall be of thee shall build the old waste places: thou shalt raise up the foundations of many generations; and thou shalt be called, The repairer of the breach, The restorer of paths to dwell in.

Isaiah 58:12

Behold, the LORD hath proclaimed unto the end of the world, Say ye to the daughter of Zion, Behold, thy salvation cometh; behold, his reward is with him, and his work before him.

Isaiah 62:11

To wit, that God was in Christ, reconciling the world unto himself, not imputing their trespasses unto them; and hath committed unto us the word of reconciliation.

II Corinthians 5:19

For ye have not received the spirit of bondage again to fear; but ye have received the Spirit of adoption, whereby we cry, Abba, Father.

Romans 8:15

For by grace are ye saved through faith; and that not of yourselves: it is the gift of God.

Ephesians 2:8

But now in Christ Jesus ye who sometimes were far off are made nigh by the blood of Christ.

Ephesians 2:13

The Lord is not slack concerning his promise, as some men count slackness; but is longsuffering to us-ward, not willing that any should perish, but that all should come to repentance.

II Peter 3:9

Therefore if any man be in Christ, he is a new creature: old things are passed away; behold, all things are become new.

II Corinthians 5:17

I am the door: by me if any man enter in, he shall be saved, and shall go in and out, and find pasture.

John 10:9

The thief cometh not, but for to steal, and to kill, and to destroy: I am come that they might have life, and that they might have it more abundantly.

John 10:10

I am the good shepherd: the good shepherd giveth his life for the sheep.

John 10:11

But he that is an hireling, and not the shepherd, whose own the sheep are not, seeth the wolf coming, and leaveth the sheep, and fleeth: and the wolf catcheth them, and scattereth the sheep.

John 10:12

The hireling fleeth, because he is an hireling, and careth not for the sheep.

John 10:13

I am the good shepherd, and know my sheep, and am known of mine.

John 10:14

As the Father knoweth me, even so know I the Father: and I lay down my life for the sheep.

John 10:15

And other sheep I have, which are not of this fold: them also I must bring, and they shall hear my voice; and there shall be one fold, and one shepherd.

John 10:16

Therefore doth my Father love me, because I lay down my life, that I might take it again.

John 10:17

Who being the brightness of his glory, and the express image of his person, and upholding all things by the word of his power, when he had by himself purged our sins, sat down on the right hand of the Majesty on high.

Hebrews 1:3

Being made so much better than the angels, as he hath by inheritance obtained a more excellent name than they.

Hebrews 1:4

For unto which of the angels said he at any time, Thou art my Son, this day have I begotten thee? And again, I will be to him a Father, and he shall be to me a Son?

Hebrews 1:5

And again, when he bringeth in the firstbegotten into the world, he saith, And let all the angels of God worship him.

Hebrews 1:6

Nevertheless death reigned from Adam to Moses, even over them that had not sinned after the similitude of Adam's transgression, who is the figure of him that was to come.

Romans 5:14

For as in Adam all die, even so in Christ shall all be made alive.

I Corinthians 15:22

And so it is written, The first man Adam was made a living soul; the last Adam was made a quickening spirit.

I Corinthians 15:45

And I heard a great voice out of heaven saying, Behold, the tabernacle of God is with men, and he will dwell with them, and they shall be his people, and God himself shall be with them, and be their God.

Revelation 21:3

What man of you, having an hundred sheep, if he lose one of them, doth not leave the ninety and nine in the wilderness, and go after that which is lost, until he find it?

Luke 15:4

Jesus saith unto him, I am the way, the truth, and the life: no man cometh unto the Father, but by me.

John 14:6

But God commendeth his love toward us, in that, while we were yet sinners, Christ died for us.

Romans 5:8

Much more then, being now justified by his blood, we shall be saved from wrath through him.

Romans 5:9

For if, when we were enemies, we were reconciled to God by the death of his Son, much more, being reconciled, we shall be saved by his life.

Romans 5:10

When Jesus heard it, he saith unto them, They that are whole have no need of the physician, but they that are sick: I came not to call the righteous, but sinners to repentance.

Mark 2:17

~ *Resurrection* ~

Jesus said unto her, I am the resurrection, and the life: he that believeth in me, though he were dead, yet shall he live.

John 11:25

But is now made manifest by the appearing of our Saviour Jesus Christ, who hath abolished death, and hath brought life and immortality to light through the gospel.

II Timothy 1:10

But they which shall be accounted worthy to obtain that world, and the resurrection from the dead, neither marry, nor are given in marriage.

Luke 20:35

Neither can they die any more: for they are equal unto the angels; and are the children of God, being the children of the resurrection.

Luke 20:36

Verily, verily, I say unto you, The hour is coming, and now is, when the dead shall hear the voice of the Son of God: and they that hear shall live.

John 5:25

And this is the Father's will which hath sent me, that of all which he hath given me I should lose nothing, but should raise it up again at the last day.

John 6:39

And this is the will of him that sent me, that every one which seeth the Son, and believeth on him, may have everlasting life: and I will raise him up at the last day.

John 6:40

No man can come to me, except the Father which hath sent me draw him: and I will raise him up at the last day.

John 6:44

And said unto them, Thus it is written, and thus it behoved Christ to suffer, and to rise from the dead the third day.

Luke 24:46

Verily, verily, I say unto you, If a man keep my saying, he shall never see death.

John 8:51

For the wages of sin is death; but the gift of God is eternal life through Jesus Christ our Lord.

Romans 6:23

I am he that liveth, and was dead; and, behold, I am alive for evermore, Amen; and have the keys of hell and of death.

Revelation 1:18

Jesus saith unto him, Go thy way; thy son liveth. And the man believed the word that Jesus had spoken unto him, and he went his way.

John 4:50

Now both the chief priests and the Pharisees had given a commandment, that, if any man knew where he were, he should shew it, that they might take him.

John 11:57

And he that was dead came forth, bound hand and foot with grave clothes: and his face was bound about with a napkin. Jesus saith unto them, Loose him, and let him go.

John 11:44

Whoso eateth my flesh, and drinketh my blood, hath eternal life; and I will raise him up at the last day.

John 6:54

So when this corruptible shall have put on incorruption, and this mortal shall have put on immortality, then shall be brought to pass the saying that is written, Death is swallowed up in victory.

I Corinthians 15:54

But God, who is rich in mercy, for his great love wherewith he loved us.

Ephesians 2:4

Even when we were dead in sins, hath quickened us together with Christ, (by grace ye are saved;)

Ephesians 2:5

And hath raised us up together, and made us sit together in heavenly places in Christ Jesus.

Ephesians 2:6

~ *Sacrifice* ~

But this man, after he had offered one sacrifice for sins for ever, sat down on the righthand of God.

Hebrews 10:12

From henceforth expecting till his enemies be made his footstool.

Hebrews 10:13

But who may abide the day of his coming? and who shall stand when he appeareth? for he is like a refiner's fire, and like fullers' soap.

Malachi 3:2

And he shall sit as a refiner and purifier of silver: and he shall purify the sons of Levi, and purge them as gold and silver, that they may offer unto the LORD an offering in righteousness.

Malachi 3:3

And as they were eating, Jesus took bread, and blessed it, and brake it, and gave it to the disciples, and said, Take, eat; this is my body.

Matthew 26:26

And he took the cup, and gave thanks, and gave it to them, saying, Drink ye all of it.

Matthew 26:27

For this is my blood of the new testament, which is shed for many for the remission of sins.

Matthew 26:28

And when he had given thanks, he brake it, and said, Take, eat: this is my body, which is broken for you: this do in remembrance of me.

I Corinthians 11:24

And walk in love, as Christ also hath loved us, and hath given himself for us an offering and a sacrifice to God for a sweetsmelling savour.

Ephesians 5:2

All we like sheep have gone astray; we have turned every one to his own way; and the LORD hath laid on him the iniquity of us all.

Isaiah 53:6

Yet it pleased the LORD to bruise him; he hath put him to grief: when thou shalt make his soul an offering for sin, he shall see his seed, he shall prolong his days, and the pleasure of the LORD shall prosper in his hand.

Isaiah 53:10

And for this cause he is the mediator of the new testament, that by means of death, for the redemption of the transgressions that were under the first testament, they which are called might receive the promise of eternal inheritance.

Hebrews 9:15

For then must he often have suffered since the foundation of the world: but now once in the end of the world hath he appeared to put away sin by the sacrifice of himself.

Hebrews 9:26

And as it is appointed unto men once to die, but after this the judgment.

Hebrews 9:27

So Christ was once offered to bear the sins of many; and unto them that look for him shall he appear the second time without sin unto salvation.

Hebrews 9:28

For this is my blood of the new testament, which is shed for many for the remission of sins.

Matthew 26:28

But if we walk in the light, as he is in the light, we have fellowship one with another, and the blood of Jesus Christ his Son cleanseth us from all sin.

I John 1:7

~ *Salvation* ~

For the Son of man is come to save that which was lost.

Matthew 18:11

How think ye? if a man have an hundred sheep, and one of them be gone astray, doth he not leave the ninety and nine, and goeth into the mountains, and seeketh that which is gone astray?

Matthew 18:12

And if so be that he find it, verily I say unto you, he rejoiceth more of that sheep, than of the ninety and nine which went not astray.

Matthew 18:13

I am the door: by me if any man enter in, he shall be saved, and shall go in and out, and find pasture.

John 10:9

The thief cometh not, but for to steal, and to kill, and to destroy: I am come that they might have life, and that they might have it more abundantly.

John 10:10

I am the good shepherd: the good shepherd giveth his life for the sheep.

John 10:11

But he that is an hireling, and not the shepherd, whose own the sheep are not, seeth the wolf coming, and leaveth the sheep, and fleeth: and the wolf catcheth them, and scattereth the sheep.

John 10:12

The hireling fleeth, because he is an hireling, and careth not for the sheep.

John 10:13

I am the good shepherd, and know my sheep, and am known of mine.

John 10:14

As the Father knoweth me, even so know I the Father: and I lay down my life for the sheep.

John 10:15

And other sheep I have, which are not of this fold: them also I must bring, and they shall hear my voice; and there shall be one fold, and one shepherd.

John 10:16

Therefore doth my Father love me, because I lay down my life, that I might take it again.

John 10:17

My sheep hear my voice, and I know them, and they follow me.

John 10:27

And I give unto them eternal life; and they shall never perish, neither shall any man pluck them out of my hand.

John 10:28

And Jesus said unto them, I am the bread of life: he that cometh to me shall never hunger; and he that believeth on me shall never thirst.

John 6:35

But I said unto you, That ye also have seen me, and believe not.

John 6:36

All that the Father giveth me shall come to me; and him that cometh to me I will in no wise cast out.

John 6:37

That whosoever believeth in him should not perish, but have eternal life.

John 3:15

For God so loved the world, that he gave his only begotten Son, that whosoever believeth in him should not perish, but have everlasting life.

John 3:16

Verily, verily, I say unto you, He that heareth my word, and believeth on him that sent me, hath everlasting life, and shall not come into condemnation; but is passed from death unto life.

John 5:24

Verily, verily, I say unto you, He that believeth on me hath everlasting life.

John 6:47

And whosoever liveth and believeth in me shall never die. Believest thou this?

John 11:26

Then said Jesus unto his disciples, If any man will come after me, let him deny himself, and take up his cross, and follow me.

Matthew 16:24

For whosoever will save his life shall lose it: and whosoever will lose his life for my sake shall find it.

Matthew 16:25

Who being the brightness of his glory, and the express image of his person, and upholding all things by the word of his power, when he had by himself purged our sins, sat down on the right hand of the Majesty on high.

Hebrews 1:3

Being made so much better than the angels, as he hath by inheritance obtained a more excellent name than they.

Hebrews 1:4

For unto which of the angels said he at any time, Thou art my Son, this day have I begotten thee? And again, I will be to him a Father, and he shall be to me a Son?

Hebrews 1:5

And again, when he bringeth in the firstbegotten into the world, he saith, And let all the angels of God worship him.

Hebrews 1:6

The Lord is not slack concerning his promise, as some men count slackness; but is longsuffering to us-ward, not willing that any should perish, but that all should come to repentance.

II Peter 3:9

The God of my rock; in him will I trust: he is my shield, and the horn of my salvation, my high tower, and my refuge, my saviour; thou savest me from violence.

II Samuel 22:3

That if thou shalt confess with thy mouth the Lord Jesus, and shalt believe in thine heart that God hath raised him from the dead, thou shalt be saved.

Romans 10:9

For the Son of man is come to seek and to save that which was lost.

Luke 19:10

I, even I, am the LORD; and beside me there is no saviour.

Isaiah 43:11

What man of you, having an hundred sheep, if he lose one of them, doth not leave the ninety and nine in the wilderness, and go after that which is lost, until he find it?

Luke 15:4

And when he hath found it, he layeth it on his shoulders, rejoicing.

Luke 15:5

And when he cometh home, he calleth together his friends and neighbours, saying unto them, Rejoice with me; for I have found my sheep which was lost.

Luke 15:6

I say unto you, that likewise joy shall be in heaven over one sinner that repenteth, more than over ninety and nine just persons, which need no repentance.

Luke 15:7

I have blotted out, as a thick cloud, thy transgressions, and, as a cloud, thy sins: return unto me; for I have redeemed thee.

Isaiah 44:22

~ *Truth* ~

Jesus saith unto him, I am the way, the truth, and the life: no man cometh unto the Father, but by me.

John 14:6

And Jesus, when he came out, saw much people, and was moved with compassion toward them, because they were as sheep not having a shepherd: and he began to teach them many things.

Mark 6:34

Then said I, Lo, I come: in the volume of the book it is written of me.

Psalms 40:7

I delight to do thy will, O my God: yea, thy law is within my heart.

Psalms 40:8

In the beginning was the Word, and the Word was with God, and the Word was God.

John 1:1

The same was in the beginning with God.

John 1:2

In him was life; and the life was the light of men.

John 1:4

John bare witness of him, and cried, saying, This was he of whom I spake, He that cometh after me is preferred before me: for he was before me.

John 1:15

And unto the angel of the church of the Laodiceans write; These things saith the Amen, the faithful and true witness, the beginning of the creation of God.

Revelation 3:14

And he said unto them, These are the words which I spake unto you, while I was yet with you, that all things must be fulfilled, which were written in the law of Moses, and in the prophets, and in the psalms, concerning me.

Luke 24:44

Heaven and earth shall pass away, but my words shall not pass away.

Matthew 24:35

(For the fruit of the Spirit is in all goodness and righteousness and truth).

Ephesians 5:9

This is he that came by water and blood, even Jesus Christ; not by water only, but by water and blood. And it is the Spirit that beareth witness, because the Spirit is truth.

I John 5:6

The world cannot hate you; but me it hateth, because I testify of it, that the works thereof are evil.

John 7:7

And from Jesus Christ, who is the faithful witness, and the first begotten of the dead, and the prince of the kings of the earth. Unto him that loved us, and washed us from our sins in his own blood.

Revelation 1:5

God's Promises through...

CHRIST'S PROVISIONS

God's Promises through...

CHRIST'S PROVISIONS

"I can do all things through Christ
which strengtheneth me"
Philippians 4:13

~ Angels ~

And again, when he bringeth in the firstbegotten into the world, he saith, And let all the angels of God worship him.

Hebrews 1:6

When the Son of man shall come in his glory, and all the holy angels with him, then shall he sit upon the throne of his glory.

Matthew 25:31

The Son of man shall send forth his angels, and they shall gather out of his kingdom all things that offend, and them which do iniquity.

Matthew 13:41

Who being the brightness of his glory, and the express image of his person, and upholding all things by the word of his power, when he had by himself purged our sins, sat down on the right hand of the Majesty on high.

Hebrews 1:3

In all their affliction he was afflicted, and the angel of his presence saved them: in his love and in his pity he redeemed them; and he bare them, and carried them all the days of old.

Isaiah 63:9

The Revelation of Jesus Christ, which God gave unto him, to shew unto his servants things which must shortly come to pass; and he sent and signified it by his angel unto his servant John.

Revelation 1:1

Then said Jesus unto him, Put up again thy sword into his place: for all they that take the sword shall perish with the sword.

Matthew 26:52

Thinkest thou that I cannot now pray to my Father, and he shall presently give me more than twelve legions of angels?

Matthew 26:53

But how then shall the scriptures be fulfilled, that thus it must be?

Matthew 26:54

And there appeared an angel unto him from heaven, strengthening him.

Luke 22:43

And, lo, the angel of the Lord came upon them, and the glory of the Lord shone round about them: and they were sore afraid.

Luke 2:9

And the angel said unto them, Fear not: for, behold, I bring you good tidings of great joy, which shall be to all people.

Luke 2:10

For unto you is born this day in the city of David a Saviour, which is Christ the Lord.

Luke 2:11

And this shall be a sign unto you; Ye shall find the babe wrapped in swaddling clothes, lying in a manger.

Luke 2:12

And suddenly there was with the angel a multitude of the heavenly host praising God, and saying.

Luke 2:13

Glory to God in the highest, and on earth peace, good will toward men.

Luke 2:14

And it came to pass, as the angels were gone away from them into heaven, the shepherds said one to another, Let us now go even unto Beth-lehem, and see this thing which is come to pass, which the Lord hath made known unto us.

Luke 2:15

And he was there in the wilderness forty days, tempted of Satan; and was with the wild beasts; and the angels ministered unto him.

Mark 1:13

And in the sixth month the angel Gabriel was sent from God unto a city of Galilee, named Nazareth,

Luke 1:26

To a virgin espoused to a man whose name was Joseph, of the house of David; and the virgin's name was Mary.

Luke 1:27

And the angel came in unto her, and said, Hail, thou that art highly favoured, the Lord is with thee: blessed art thou among women.

Luke 1:28

And when she saw him, she was troubled at his saying, and cast in her mind what manner of salutation this should be.

Luke 1:29

And the angel said unto her, Fear not, Mary: for thou hast found favour with God.

Luke 1:30

And, behold, thou shalt conceive in thy womb, and bring forth a son, and shalt call his me JESUS.

Luke 1:31

He shall be great, and shall be called the Son of the Highest: and the Lord God shall give unto him the throne of his father David.

Luke 1:32

And he shall reign over the house of Jacob for ever; and of his kingdom there shall be no end.

Luke 1:33

Then said Mary unto the angel, How shall this be, seeing I know not a man?

Luke 1:34

And the angel answered and said unto her, The Holy Ghost shall come upon thee, and the power of the Highest shall overshadow thee: therefore also that holy thing which shall be born of thee shall be called the Son of God.

Luke 1:35

~ *Anointing* ~

And they were astonished at his doctrine: for he taught them as one that had authority, and not as the scribes.

Mark 1:22

And Jesus, when he was baptized, went up straightway out of the water: and, lo, the heavens were opened unto him, and he saw the Spirit of God descending like a dove, and lighting upon him.

Matthew 3:16

And lo a voice from heaven, saying, This is my beloved Son, in whom I am well pleased.

Matthew 3:17

And Jesus returned in the power of the Spirit into Galilee: and there went out a fame of him through all the region round about.

Luke 4:14

He first findeth his own brother Simon, and saith unto him, We have found the Messias, which is, being interpreted, the Christ.

John 1:41

For he whom God hath sent speaketh the words of God: for God giveth not the Spirit by measure unto him.

John 3:34

The Father loveth the Son, and hath given all things into his hand.

John 3:35

Who by the mouth of thy servant David hast said, Why did the heathen rage, and the people imagine vain things?

Acts 4:25

The kings of the earth stood up, and the rulers were gathered together against the Lord, and against his Christ.

Acts 4:26

For of a truth against thy holy child Jesus, whom thou hast anointed, both Herod, and Pontius Pilate, with the Gentiles, and the people of Israel, were gathered together.

Acts 4:27

How God anointed Jesus of Nazareth with the Holy Ghost and with power: who went about doing good, and healing all that were oppressed of the devil; for God was with him.

Acts 10:38

~ Birth ~

For unto which of the angels said he at any time, Thou art my Son, this day have I begotten thee? And again, I will be to him a Father, and he shall be to me a Son?

Hebrews 1:5

So also Christ glorified not himself to be made an high priest; but he that said unto him, Thou art my Son, to day have I begotten thee.

Hebrews 5:5

And the Word was made flesh, and dwelt among us, (and we beheld his glory, the glory as of the only begotten of the Father,) full of grace and truth.

John 1:14

And in the sixth month the angel Gabriel was sent from God unto a city of Galilee, named Nazareth.

Luke 1:26

To a virgin espoused to a man whose name was Joseph, of the house of David; and the virgin's name was Mary.

Luke 1:27

And the angel came in unto her, and said, Hail, thou that art highly favoured, the Lord is with thee: blessed art thou among women.

Luke 1:28

And when she saw him, she was troubled at his saying, and cast in her mind what manner of salutation this should be.

Luke 1:29

And the angel said unto her, Fear not, Mary: for thou hast found favour with God.

Luke 1:30

And he shall reign over the house of Jacob for ever; and of his kingdom there shall be no end.

Luke 1:33

Then said Mary unto the angel, How shall this be, seeing I know not a man?

Luke 1:34

And the angel answered and said unto her, The Holy Ghost shall come upon thee, and the power of the Highest shall overshadow thee: therefore also that holy thing which shall be born of thee shall be called the Son of God.

Luke 1:35

And she shall bring forth a son, and thou shalt call his name JESUS: for he shall save his people from their sins.

Matthew 1:21

And, behold, thou shalt conceive in thy womb, and bring forth a son, and shalt call his name JESUS.

Luke 1:31

He shall be great, and shall be called the Son of the Highest: and the Lord God shall give unto him the throne of his father David.

Luke 1:32

John answered and said, A man can receive nothing, except it be given him from heaven.

John 3:27

And no man taketh this honour unto himself, but he that is called of God, as was Aaron.

Hebrews 5:4

Behold my servant, whom I have chosen; my beloved, in whom my soul is well pleased: I will put my spirit upon him, and he shall shew judgment to the Gentiles.

Matthew 12:18

For unto us a child is born, unto us a son is given: and the government shall be upon his shoulder: and his name shall be called Wonderful, Counsellor, The mighty God, The everlasting Father, The Prince of Peace.

Isaiah 9:6

Therefore the Lord himself shall give you a sign; Behold, a virgin shall conceive, and bear a son, and shall call his name Immanuel.

Isaiah 7:14

And again, when he bringeth in the firstbegotten into the world, he saith, And let all the angels of God worship him.

Hebrews 1:6

~ *Blood* ~

For this is my blood of the new testament, which is shed for many for the remission of sins.

Matthew 26:28

But he was wounded for our transgressions, he was bruised for our iniquities: the chastisement of our peace was upon him; and with his stripes we are healed.

Isaiah 53:5

For if, when we were enemies, we were reconciled to God by the death of his Son, much more, being reconciled, we shall be saved by his life.

Romans 5:10

And not only so, but we also joy in God through our Lord Jesus Christ, by whom we have now received the atonement.

Romans 5:11

And the blood shall be to you for a token upon the houses where ye are: and when I see the blood, I will pass over you, and the plague shall not be upon you to destroy you, when I smite the land of Egypt.

Exodus 12:13

Take heed therefore unto yourselves, and to all the flock, over the which the Holy Ghost hath made you overseers, to feed the church of God, which he hath purchased with his own blood.

Acts 20:28

How much more shall the blood of Christ, who through the eternal Spirit offered himself without spot to God, purge your conscience from dead works to serve the living God?

Hebrews 9:14

But now in Christ Jesus ye who sometimes were far off are made nigh by the blood of Christ.

Ephesians 2:13

Likewise also the cup after supper, saying, This cup is the new testament in my blood, which is shed for you.

Luke 22:20

And from Jesus Christ, who is the faithful witness, and the first begotten of the dead, and the prince of the kings of the earth. Unto him that loved us, and washed us from our sins in his own blood,

Revelation 1:5

~ *Brightness* ~

I Jesus have sent mine angel to testify unto you these things in the churches. I am the root and the offspring of David, and the bright and morning star.

Revelation 22:16

Then spake Jesus again unto them, saying, I am the light of the world: he that followeth me shall not walk in darkness, but shall have the light of life.

John 8:12

Then Jesus said unto them, Yet a little while is the light with you. Walk while ye have the light, lest darkness come upon you: for he that walketh in darkness knoweth not whither he goeth.

John 12:35

While ye have light, believe in the light, that ye may be the children of light. These things spake Jesus, and departed, and did hide himself from them.

John 12:36

I am come a light into the world, that whosoever believeth on me should not abide in darkness.

John 12:46

As long as I am in the world, I am the light of the world.

John 9:5

And unto the angel of the church in Thyatira write; These things saith the Son of God, who hath his eyes like unto a flame of fire, and his feet are like fine brass;

Revelation 2:18

But unto you that fear my name shall the Sun of righteousness arise with healing in his wings; and ye shall go forth, and grow up as calves of the stall.

Malachi 4:2

A light to lighten the Gentiles, and the glory of thy people Israel.

Luke 2:32

That was the true Light, which lighteth every man that cometh into the world.

John 1:9

For God, who commanded the light to shine out of darkness, hath shined in our hearts, to give the light of the knowledge of the glory of God in the face of Jesus Christ.

II Corinthians 4:6

Again, a new commandment I write unto you, which thing is true in him and in you: because the darkness is past, and the true light now shineth.

I John 2:8

~ *Compassion* ~

Then said Jesus, Father, forgive them; for they know not what they do. And they parted his raiment, and cast lots.

Luke 23:34

So Jesus had compassion on them, and touched their eyes: and immediately their eyes received sight, and they followed him.

Matthew 20:34

And Jesus, moved with compassion, put forth his hand, and touched him, and saith unto him, I will; be thou clean.

Mark 1:41

And when the scribes and Pharisees saw him eat with publicans and sinners, they said unto his disciples, How is it that he eateth and drinketh with publicans and sinners?

Mark 2:16

When Jesus heard it, he saith unto them, They that are whole have no need of the physician, but they that are sick: I came not to call the righteous, but sinners to repentance.

Mark 2:17

And Jesus, when he came out, saw much people, and was moved with compassion toward them, because they were as sheep not having a shepherd: and he began to teach them many things.

Mark 6:34

And when he heard that it was Jesus of Nazareth, he began to cry out, and say, Jesus, thou son of David, have mercy on me.

Mark 10:47

And many charged him that he should hold his peace: but he cried the more a great deal, Thou son of David, have mercy on me.

Mark 10:48

And Jesus stood still, and commanded him to be called. And they call the blind man, saying unto him, Be of good comfort, rise; he calleth thee.

Mark 10:49

~ *Dominion* ~

I saw in the night visions, and, behold, one like the Son of man came with the clouds of heaven, and came to the Ancient of days, and they brought him near before him.

Daniel 7:13

And there was given him dominion, and glory, and a kingdom, that all people, nations, and languages, should serve him: his dominion is an everlasting dominion, which shall not pass away, and his kingdom that which shall not be destroyed.

Daniel 7:14

If ye then be risen with Christ, seek those things which are above, where Christ sitteth on the right hand of God.

Colossians 3:1

And, behold, thou shalt conceive in thy womb, and bring forth a son, and shalt call his name JESUS.

Luke 1:31

He shall be great, and shall be called the Son of the Highest: and the Lord God shall give unto him the throne of his father David.

Luke 1:32

And he shall reign over the house of Jacob for ever; and of his kingdom there shall be no end.

Luke 1:33

Saying, Let us alone; what have we to do with thee, thou Jesus of Nazareth? art thou come to destroy us? I know thee who thou art, the Holy One of God.

Mark 1:24

And Jesus rebuked him, saying, Hold thy peace, and come out of him.

Mark 1:25

And when the unclean spirit had torn him, and cried with a loud voice, he came out of him.

Mark 1:26

And they were all amazed, insomuch that they questioned among themselves, saying, What thing is this? what new doctrine is this? for with authority commandeth he even the unclean spirits, and they do obey him.

Mark 1:27

For by him were all things created, that are in heaven, and that are in earth, visible and invisible, whether they be thrones, or dominions, or principalities, or powers: all things were created by him, and for him.

Colossians 1:16

And he is before all things, and by him all things consist.

Colossians 1:17

That at the name of Jesus every knee should bow, of things in heaven, and things in earth, and things under the earth.

Philippians 2:10

Who being the brightness of his glory, and the express image of his person, and upholding all things by the word of his power, when he had by himself purged our sins, sat down on the right hand of the Majesty on high.

Hebrews 1:3

Then cometh the end, when he shall have delivered up the kingdom to God, even the Father; when he shall have put down all rule and all authority and power.

I Corinthians 15:24

For he hath put all things under his feet. But when he saith all things are put under him, it is manifest that he is excepted, which did put all things under him.

I Corinthians 15:27

A Psalm of David. The LORD said unto my Lord, Sit thou at my right hand, until I make thine enemies thy footstool.

Psalms 110:1

This is the stone which was set at nought of you builders, which is become the head of the corner.

Acts 4:11

Neither is there salvation in any other: for there is none other name under heaven given among men, whereby we must be saved.

Acts 4:12

~ *Father* ~

He shall be great, and shall be called the Son of the Highest: and the Lord God shall give unto him the throne of his father David.

Luke 1:32

And the glory which thou gavest me I have given them; that they may be one, even as we are one.

John 17:22

Father, I will that they also, whom thou hast given me, be with me where I am; that they may behold my glory, which thou hast given me: for thou lovedst me before the foundation of the world.

John 17:24

O righteous Father, the world hath not known thee: but I have known thee, and these have known that thou hast sent me.

John 17:25

And I have declared unto them thy name, and will declare it: that the love wherewith thou hast loved me may be in them, and I in them.

John 17:26

And now, O Father, glorify thou me with thine own self with the glory which I had with thee before the world was.

John 17:5

And straightway coming up out of the water, he saw the heavens opened, and the Spirit like a dove descending upon him.

Mark 1:10

And there came a voice from heaven, saying, Thou art my beloved Son, in whom I am well pleased.

Mark 1:11

And the angel answered and said unto her, The Holy Ghost shall come upon thee, and the power of the Highest shall overshadow thee: therefore also that holy thing which shall be born of thee shall be called the Son of God.

Luke 1:35

That all men should honour the Son, even as they honour the Father. He that honoureth not the Son honoureth not the Father which hath sent him.

John 5:23

I am Alpha and Omega, the beginning and the ending, saith the Lord, which is, and which was, and which is to come, the Almighty.

Revelation 1:8

I will not leave you comfortless: I will come to you.

John 14:18

Yet a little while, and the world seeth me no more; but ye see me: because I live, ye shall live also.

John 14:19

Who is the image of the invisible God, the first-born of every creature.

Colossians 1:15

~ *God* ~

I and my Father are one.

John 10:30

And Jesus said unto him, Thou hast both seen him, and it is he that talketh with thee.

John 9:37

And now, O Father, glorify thou me with thine own self with the glory which I had with thee before the world was.

John 17:5

And Jesus answered and said, while he taught in the temple, How say the scribes that Christ is the son of David?

Mark 12:35

For David himself said by the Holy Ghost, The Lord said to my Lord, Sit thou on my right hand, till I make thine enemies thy footstool.

Mark 12:36

David therefore himself calleth him Lord; and whence is he then his son? And the common people heard him gladly.

Mark 12:37

I said therefore unto you, that ye shall die in your sins: for if ye believe not that I am he, ye shall die in your sins.

John 8:24

Your father Abraham rejoiced to see my day: and he saw it, and was glad.

John 8:56

Jesus said unto them, Verily, verily, I say unto you, Before Abraham was, I am.

John 8:58

I am Alpha and Omega, the beginning and the ending, saith the Lord, which is, and which was, and which is to come, the Almighty.

Revelation 1:8

In the beginning was the Word, and the Word was with God, and the Word was God.

John 1:1

Looking for that blessed hope, and the glorious appearing of the great God and our Saviour Jesus Christ.

Titus 2:13

Not that any man hath seen the Father, save he which is of God, he hath seen the Father.

John 6:46

Then said Jesus unto them, Yet a little while am I with you, and then I go unto him that sent me.

John 7:33

And he said, Therefore said I unto you, that no man can come unto me, except it were given unto him of my Father.

John 6:65

If I do not the works of my Father, believe me not.

John 10:37

But if I do, though ye believe not me, believe the works: that ye may know, and believe, that the Father is in me, and I in him.

John 10:38

For the Father loveth the Son, and sheweth him all things that himself doeth: and he will shew him greater works than these, that ye may marvel.

John 5:20

~ *Immortality* ~

Jesus Christ the same yesterday, and to day, and for ever.

Hebrews 13:8

And he saith unto them, Be not affrighted: Ye seek Jesus of Nazareth, which was crucified: he is risen; he is not here: behold the place where they laid him.

Mark 16:6

I am Alpha and Omega, the beginning and the ending, saith the Lord, which is, and which was, and which is to come, the Almighty.

Revelation 1:8

And unto the angel of the church in Smyrna write; These things saith the first and the last, which was dead, and is alive.

Revelation 2:8

Who verily was foreordained before the foundation of the world, but was manifest in these last times for you.

I Peter 1:20

And now, O Father, glorify thou me with thine own self with the glory which I had with thee before the world was.

John 17:5

And he is before all things, and by him all things consist.

Colossians 1:17

Hath in these last days spoken unto us by his Son, whom he hath appointed heir of all things, by whom also he made the worlds.

Hebrews 1:2

And, Thou, Lord, in the beginning hast laid the foundation of the earth; and the heavens are the works of thine hands.

Hebrews 1:10

I saw in the night visions, and, behold, one like the Son of man came with the clouds of heaven, and came to the Ancient of days, and they brought him near before him.

Daniel 7:13

And there was given him dominion, and glory, and a kingdom, that all people, nations, and languages, should serve him: his dominion is an everlasting dominion, which shall not pass away, and his kingdom that which shall not be destroyed.

Daniel 7:14

And God said, Let us make man in our image, after our likeness: and let them have dominion over the fish of the sea, and over the fowl of the air, and over the cattle, and over all the earth, and over every creeping thing that creepeth upon the earth.

Genesis 1:26

~ Judge ~

For we must all appear before the judgment seat of Christ; that every one may receive the things done in his body, according to that he hath done, whether it be good or bad.

II Corinthians 5:10

For the Father judgeth no man, but hath committed all judgment unto the Son.

John 5:22

That all men should honour the Son, even as they honour the Father. He that honoureth not the Son honoureth not the Father which hath sent him.

John 5:23

Who shall give account to him that is ready to judge the quick and the dead.

I Peter 4:5

And Enoch also, the seventh from Adam, prophesied of these, saying, Behold, the Lord cometh with ten thousands of his saints.

Jude 1:14

To execute judgment upon all, and to convince all that are ungodly among them of all their ungodly deeds which they have ungodly committed, and of all their hard speeches which ungodly sinners have spoken against him.

Jude 1:15

And I heard another out of the altar say, Even so, Lord God Almighty, true and righteous are thy judgments.

Revelation 16:7

For true and righteous are his judgments: for he hath judged the great whore, which did corrupt the earth with her fornication, and hath avenged the blood of his servants at her hand.

Revelation 19:2

And there shall come forth a rod out of the stem of Jesse, and a Branch shall grow out of his roots.

Isaiah 11:1

And he shall sit as a refiner and purifier of silver: and he shall purify the sons of Levi, and purge them as gold and silver, that they may offer unto the LORD an offering in righteousness.

Malachi 3:3

And now also the axe is laid unto the root of the trees: therefore every tree which bringeth not forth good fruit is hewn down, and cast into the fire.

Matthew 3:10

I indeed baptize you with water unto repentance: but he that cometh after me is mightier than I, whose shoes I am not worthy to bear: he shall baptize you with the Holy Ghost, and with fire.

Matthew 3:11

Whose fan is in his hand, and he will throughly purge his floor, and gather his wheat into the garner; but he will burn up the chaff with unquenchable fire.

Matthew 3:12

For our God is a consuming fire.

Hebrews 12:29

~ *King* ~

Behold, the days come, saith the LORD, that I will raise unto David a righteous Branch, and a King shall reign and prosper, and shall execute judgment and justice in the earth.

Jeremiah 23:5

When the Son of man shall come in his glory, and all the holy angels with him, then shall he sit upon the throne of his glory:

Matthew 25:31

And before him shall be gathered all nations: and he shall separate them one from another, as a shepherd divideth his sheep from the goats:

Matthew 25:32

And he shall set the sheep on his right hand, but the goats on the left.

Matthew 25:33

Then shall the King say unto them on his right hand, Come, ye blessed of my Father, inherit the kingdom prepared for you from the foundation of the world.

Matthew 25:34

I saw in the night visions, and, behold, one like the Son of man came with the clouds of heaven, and came to the Ancient of days, and they brought him near before him.

Daniel 7:13

And there was given him dominion, and glory, and a kingdom, that all people, nations, and languages, should serve him: his dominion is an everlasting dominion, which shall not pass away, and his kingdom that which shall not be destroyed.

Daniel 7:14

They shall fear thee as long as the sun and moon endure, throughout all generations.

Psalms 72:5

He shall have dominion also from sea to sea, and from the river unto the ends of the earth.

Psalms 72:8

Yea, all kings shall fall down before him: all nations shall serve him.

Psalms 72:11

Pilate therefore said unto him, Art thou a king then? Jesus answered, Thou sayest that I am a king. To this end was I born, and for this cause came I into the world, that I should bear witness unto the truth. Every one that is of the truth heareth my voice.

John 18:37

Jesus saith unto him, Thou hast said: nevertheless I say unto you, Hereafter shall ye see the Son of man sitting on the right hand of power, and coming in the clouds of heaven.

Matthew 26:64

But we speak the wisdom of God in a mystery, even the hidden wisdom, which God ordained before the world unto our glory.

I Corinthians 2:7

Which none of the princes of this world knew: for had they known it, they would not have crucified the Lord of glory.

I Corinthians 2:8

Who being the brightness of his glory, and the express image of his person, and upholding all things by the word of his power, when he had by himself purged our sins, sat down on the right hand of the Majesty on high.

Hebrews 1:3

Now unto the King eternal, immortal, invisible, the only wise God, be honour and glory for ever and ever. Amen.

I Timothy 1:17

~ *Lamb* ~

And I beheld, and I heard the voice of many angels round about the throne and the beasts and the elders: and the number of them was ten thousand times ten thousand, and thousands of thousands.

Revelation 5:11

Saying with a loud voice, Worthy is the Lamb that was slain to receive power, and riches, and wisdom, and strength, and honour, and glory, and blessing.

Revelation 5:12

And every creature which is in heaven, and on the earth, and under the earth, and such as are in the sea, and all that are in them, heard I saying, Blessing, and honour, and glory, and power, be unto him that sitteth upon the throne, and unto the Lamb for ever and ever.

Revelation 5:13

And the four beasts said, Amen. And the four and twenty elders fell down and worshipped him that liveth for ever and ever.

Revelation 5:14

All we like sheep have gone astray; we have turned every one to his own way; and the LORD hath laid on him the iniquity of us all.

Isaiah 53:6

He was oppressed, and he was afflicted, yet he opened not his mouth: he is brought as a lamb to the slaughter, and as a sheep before her shearers is dumb, so he openeth not his mouth.

Isaiah 53:7

He was taken from prison and from judgment: and who shall declare his generation? for he was cut off out of the land of the living: for the transgression of my people was he stricken.

Isaiah 53:8

And he made his grave with the wicked, and with the rich in his death; because he had done no violence, neither was any deceit in his mouth.

Isaiah 53:9

Yet it pleased the LORD to bruise him; he hath put him to grief: when thou shalt make his soul an offering for sin, he shall see his seed, he shall prolong his days, and the pleasure of the LORD shall prosper in his hand.

Isaiah 53:10

He shall see of the travail of his soul, and shall be satisfied: by his knowledge shall my righteous servant justify many; for he shall bear their iniquities.

Isaiah 53:11

The next day John seeth Jesus coming unto him, and saith, Behold the Lamb of God, which taketh away the sin of the world.

John 1:29

Purge out therefore the old leaven, that ye may be a new lump, as ye are unleavened. For even Christ our passover is sacrificed for us.

I Corinthians 5:7

And walk in love, as Christ also hath loved us, and hath given himself for us an offering and a sacrifice to God for a sweetsmelling savour.

Ephesians 5:2

Forasmuch as ye know that ye were not redeemed with corruptible things, as silver and gold, from your vain conversation received by tradition from your fathers.

I Peter 1:18

But with the precious blood of Christ, as of a lamb without blemish and without spot. .

I Peter 1:19

Looking unto Jesus the author and finisher of our faith; who for the joy that was set before him endured the cross, despising the shame, and is set down at the right hand of the throne of God.

Hebrews 12:2

And all that dwell upon the earth shall worship him, whose names are not written in the book of life of the Lamb slain from the foundation of the world.

Revelation 13:8

~ *Lord* ~

Wherefore God also hath highly exalted him, and given him a name which is above every name:

Philippians 2:9

That at the name of Jesus every knee should bow, of things in heaven, and things in earth, and things under the earth.

Philippians 2:10

And that every tongue should confess that Jesus Christ is Lord, to the glory of God the Father.

Philippians 2:11

And I, if I be lifted up from the earth, will draw all men unto me.

John 12:32

Therefore the Son of man is Lord also of the sabbath.

Mark 2:28

Who being the brightness of his glory, and the express image of his person, and upholding all things by the word of his power, when he had by himself purged our sins, sat down on the right hand of the Majesty on high.

Hebrews 1:3

And Thomas answered and said unto him, My Lord and my God.

John 20:28

For unto you is born this day in the city of David a Saviour, which is Christ the Lord.

Luke 2:11

Masters, give unto your servants that which is just and equal; knowing that ye also have a Master in heaven.

Colossians 4:1

But be not ye called Rabbi: for one is your Master, even Christ; and all ye are brethren.

Matthew 23:8

Jesus answered, My kingdom is not of this world: if my kingdom were of this world, then would my servants fight, that I should not be delivered to the Jews: but now is my kingdom not from hence.

John 18:36

Pilate therefore said unto him, Art thou a king then? Jesus answered, Thou sayest that I am a king. To this end was I born, and for this cause came I into the world, that I should bear witness unto the truth. Every one that is of the truth heareth my voice.

John 18:37

~ Love ~

But when he saw the multitudes, he was moved with compassion on them, because they fainted, and were scattered abroad, as sheep having no shepherd.

Matthew 9:36

This is my commandment, That ye love one another, as I have loved you.

John 15:12

Then said Jesus unto Peter, Put up thy sword into the sheath: the cup which my Father hath given me, shall I not drink it?

John 18:11

For where two or three are gathered together in my name, there am I in the midst of them.

Matthew 18:20

For the Lamb which is in the midst of the throne shall feed them, and shall lead them unto living fountains of waters: and God shall wipe away all tears from their eyes.

Revelation 7:17

But God commendeth his love toward us, in that, while we were yet sinners, Christ died for us.

Romans 5:8

And walk in love, as Christ also hath loved us, and hath given himself for us an offering and a sacrifice to God for a sweetsmelling savour.

Ephesians 5:2

But after that the kindness and love of God our Saviour toward man appeared.

Titus 3:4

Let your conversation be without covetousness; and be content with such things as ye have: for he hath said, I will never leave thee, nor forsake thee.

Hebrews 13:5

For I am persuaded, that neither death, nor life, nor angels, nor principalities, nor powers, nor things present, nor things to come.

Romans 8:38

Nor height, nor depth, nor any other creature, shall be able to separate us from the love of God, which is in Christ Jesus our Lord.

Romans 8:39

~ *Messiahship* ~

All we like sheep have gone astray; we have turned every one to his own way; and the LORD hath laid on him the iniquity of us all.

Isaiah 53:6

He was oppressed, and he was afflicted, yet he opened not his mouth: he is brought as a lamb to the slaughter, and as a sheep before her shearers is dumb, so he openeth not his mouth.

Isaiah 53:7

He was taken from prison and from judgment: and who shall declare his generation? for he was cut off out of the land of the living: for the transgression of my people was he stricken.

Isaiah 53:8

And he made his grave with the wicked, and with the rich in his death; because he had done no violence, neither was any deceit in his mouth.

Isaiah 53:9

Yet it pleased the LORD to bruise him; he hath put him to grief: when thou shalt make his soul an offering for sin, he shall see his seed, he shall prolong his days, and the pleasure of the LORD shall prosper in his hand.

Isaiah 53:10

He shall see of the travail of his soul, and shall be satisfied: by his knowledge shall my righteous servant justify many; for he shall bear their iniquities.

Isaiah 53:11

Therefore will I divide him a portion with the great, and he shall divide the spoil with the strong; because he hath poured out his soul unto death: and he was numbered with the transgressors; and he bare the sin of many, and made intercession for the transgressors.

Isaiah 53:12

If the Son therefore shall make you free, ye shall be free indeed.

John 8:36

The Spirit of the Lord is upon me, because he hath anointed me to preach the gospel to the poor; he hath sent me to heal the brokenhearted, to preach deliverance to the captives, and recovering of sight to the blind, to set at liberty them that are bruised,

Luke 4:18

To preach the acceptable year of the Lord.

Luke 4:19

For the Son of man is come to seek and to save that which was lost.

Luke 19:10

I am the good shepherd: the good shepherd giveth his life for the sheep.

John 10:11

Forasmuch as ye know that ye were not redeemed with corruptible things, as silver and gold, from your vain conversation received by tradition from your fathers.

I Peter 1:18

But with the precious blood of Christ, as of a lamb without blemish and without spot.

I Peter 1:19

Who verily was foreordained before the foundation of the world, but was manifest in these last times for you.

I Peter 1:20

And so all Israel shall be saved: as it is written, There shall come out of Sion the Deliverer, and shall turn away ungodliness from Jacob.

Romans 11:26

Jesus saith unto him, I am the way, the truth, and the life: no man cometh unto the Father, but by me.

John 14:6

For Christ is not entered into the holy places made with hands, which are the figures of the true; but into heaven itself, now to appear in the presence of God for us.

Hebrews 9:24

My little children, these things write I unto you, that ye sin not. And if any man sin, we have an advocate with the Father, Jesus Christ the righteous.

I John 2:1

And said unto him, Art thou he that should come, or do we look for another?

Matthew 11:3

The woman saith unto him, I know that Messias cometh, which is called Christ: when he is come, he will tell us all things.

John 4:25

And the multitudes that went before, and that followed, cried, saying, Hosanna to the son of David: Blessed is he that cometh in the name of the Lord; Hosanna in the highest.

Matthew 21:9

Looking unto Jesus the author and finisher of our faith; who for the joy that was set before him endured the cross, despising the shame, and is set down at the right hand of the throne of God.

Hebrews 12:2

But Jesus withdrew himself with his disciples to the sea: and a great multitude from Galilee followed him, and from Judaea.

Mark 3:7

And u... down before h... of God.

... when they saw him, fell ... saying, Thou art the Son

Mark 3:11

And they said, Some say that ... Baptist: some, Elias; and others, Jeremi... ... the prophets.

Matthew 1...

He saith unto them, But whom say ye that I am?
Matthew 16:15

And Simon Peter answered and said, Thou art the Christ, the Son of the living God.
Matthew 16:16

And Jesus answered and said unto him, Blessed art thou, Simon Bar-jona: for flesh and blood hath not revealed it unto thee, but my Father which is in heaven.
Matthew 16:17

And I say also unto thee, That thou art Peter, and upon this rock I will build my church; and the gates of hell shall not prevail against it.
Matthew 16:18

Jesus answered them and said, Verily, verily, I say unto you, Ye seek me, not because ye saw the miracles, but because ye did eat of the loaves, and were filled.

John 6:26

~ Power

And Jesus put forth ... and touched him, saying, I will; be ... And immediately his leprosy was cle...

Matthew 8:3

...en the even was come, they brought unto him many that were possessed with devils: and he cast out the spirits with his word, and healed all that were sick.

Matthew 8:16

That it might be fulfilled which was spoken by Esaias the prophet, saying, Himself took our infirmities, and bare our sicknesses.

Matthew 8:17

Jesus saith unto him, Thou hast said: nevertheless I say unto you, Hereafter shall ye see the Son of man sitting on the right hand of power, and coming in the clouds of heaven.

Matthew 26:64

And Jesus came and spake unto them, saying, All power is given unto me in heaven and in earth.

Matthew 28:18

I indeed have baptized you with water: but he shall baptize you with the Holy Ghost.

Mark 1:8

And he came and took her by the hand, and lifted her up; and immediately the fever left her, and she ministered unto them.

Mark 1:31

And at even, when the sun did set, they brought unto him all that were diseased, and them that were possessed with devils.

Mark 1:32

And all the city was gathered together at the door.

Mark 1:33

And he healed many that were sick of divers diseases, and cast out many devils; and suffered not the devils to speak, because they knew him.

Mark 1:34

When they saw the star, they rejoiced with exceeding great joy.

Matthew 2:10

And he arose, and rebuked the wind, and said unto the sea, Peace, be still. And the wind ceased, and there was a great calm.

Mark 4:39

But when they saw him walking upon the sea, they supposed it had been a spirit, and cried out.

Mark 6:49

For they all saw him, and were troubled. And immediately he talked with them, and saith unto them, {Be of good cheer: it is I; be not afraid.}

Mark 6:50

And when they were come out of the ship, straightway they knew him.

Mark 6:54

And ran through that whole region round about, and began to carry about in beds those that were sick, where they heard he was.

Mark 6:55

And whithersoever he entered, into villages, or cities, or country, they laid the sick in the streets, and besought him that they might touch if it were but the border of his garment: and as many as touched him were made whole.

Mark 6:56

~ *Pre-Existence* ~

And now, O Father, glorify thou me with thine own self with the glory which I had with thee before the world was.

John 17:5

Father, I will that they also, whom thou hast given me, be with me where I am; that they may behold my glory, which thou hast given me: for thou lovedst me before the foundation of the world.

John 17:24

O righteous Father, the world hath not known thee: but I have known thee, and these have known that thou hast sent me.

John 17:25

And he said unto them, Ye are from beneath; I am from above: ye are of this world; I am not of this world.

John 8:23

Jesus said unto them, Verily, verily, I say unto you, Before Abraham was, I am.

John 8:58

And he is before all things, and by him all things consist.

Colossians 1:17

Who hath saved us, and called us with an holy calling, not according to our works, but according to his own purpose and grace, which was given us in Christ Jesus before the world began.

II Timothy 1:9

Who verily was foreordained before the foundation of the world, but was manifest in these last times for you.

I Peter 1:20

I am Alpha and Omega, the beginning and the end, the first and the last.

Revelation 22:13

Hath in these last days spoken unto us by his Son, whom he hath appointed heir of all things, by whom also he made the worlds.

Hebrews 1:2

And, Thou, Lord, in the beginning hast laid the foundation of the earth; and the heavens are the works of thine hands.

Hebrews 1:10

~ *Prince* ~

For unto us a child is born, unto us a son is given: and the government shall be upon his shoulder: and his name shall be called Wonderful, Counsellor, The mighty God, The everlasting Father, The Prince of Peace.

Isaiah 9:6

Of the increase of his government and peace there shall be no end, upon the throne of David, and upon his kingdom, to order it, and to establish it with judgment and with justice from henceforth even for ever. The zeal of the LORD of hosts will perform this.

Isaiah 9:7

And killed the Prince of life, whom God hath raised from the dead; whereof we are witnesses.

Acts 3:15

Him hath God exalted with his right hand to be a Prince and a Saviour, for to give repentance to Israel, and forgiveness of sins.

Acts 5:31

For it became him, for whom are all things, and by whom are all things, in bringing many sons unto glory, to make the captain of their salvation perfect through sufferings.

Hebrews 2:10

Looking unto Jesus the author and finisher of our faith; who for the joy that was set before him endured the cross, despising the shame, and is set down at the right hand of the throne of God.

Hebrews 12:2

And from Jesus Christ, who is the faithful witness, and the first begotten of the dead, and the prince of the kings of the earth. Unto him that loved us, and washed us from our sins in his own blood.

Revelation 1:5

Know therefore and understand, that from the going forth of the commandment to restore and to build Jerusalem unto the Messiah the Prince shall be seven weeks, and threescore and two weeks: the street shall be built again, and the wall, even in troublous times.

Daniel 9:25

Behold, I have given him for a witness to the people, a leader and commander to the people.

Isaiah 55:4

That the blood of all the prophets, which was shed from the foundation of the world, may be required of this generation.

Luke 11:50

And all that dwell upon the earth shall worship him, whose names are not written in the book of life of the Lamb slain from the foundation of the world.

Revelation 13:8

And God said, Let us make man in our image, after our likeness: and let them have dominion over the fish of the sea, and over the fowl of the air, and over the cattle, and over all the earth, and over every creeping thing that creepeth upon the earth.

Genesis 1:26

I was set up from everlasting, from the beginning, or ever the earth was.

Proverbs 8:23

When there were no depths, I was brought forth; when there were no fountains abounding with water.

Proverbs 8:24

Before the mountains were settled, before the hills was I brought forth.

Proverbs 8:25

While as yet he had not made the earth, nor the fields, nor the highest part of the dust of the world.

Proverbs 8:26

~ *Wisdom* ~

Pilate therefore said unto him, Art thou a king then? Jesus answered, Thou sayest that I am a king. To this end was I born, and for this cause came I into the world, that I should bear witness unto the truth. Every one that is of the truth heareth my voice.

John 18:37

And when the sabbath day was come, he began to teach in the synagogue: and many hearing him were astonished, saying, From whence hath this man these things? and what wisdom is this which is given unto him, that even such mighty works are wrought by his hands?

Mark 6:2

But unto them which are called, both Jews and Greeks, Christ the power of God, and the wisdom of God.

I Corinthians 1:24

Because the foolishness of God is wiser than men; and the weakness of God is stronger than men.

I Corinthians 1:25

For ye see your calling, brethren, how that not many wise men after the flesh, not many mighty, not many noble, are called.

I Corinthians 1:26

But God hath chosen the foolish things of the world to confound the wise; and God hath chosen the weak things of the world to confound the things which are mighty.

I Corinthians 1:27

And base things of the world, and things which are despised, hath God chosen, yea, and things which are not, to bring to nought things that are.

I Corinthians 1:28

That no flesh should glory in his presence.

I Corinthians 1:29

But of him are ye in Christ Jesus, who of God is made unto us wisdom, and righteousness, and sanctification, and redemption.

I Corinthians 1:30

But we speak the wisdom of God in a mystery, even the hidden wisdom, which God ordained before the world unto our glory.

I Corinthians 2:7

Which none of the princes of this world knew: for had they known it, they wouldnot have crucified the Lord of glory.

I Corinthians 2:8

The queen of the south shall rise up in the judgment with the men of this generation, and condemn them: for she came from the utmost parts of the earth to hear the wisdom of Solomon; and, behold, a greater than Solomon is here.

Luke 11:31

In whom are hid all the treasures of wisdom and knowledge.

Colossians 2:3

I was set up from everlasting, from the beginning, or ever the earth was.

Proverbs 8:23

When there were no depths, I was brought forth; when there were no fountains abounding with water.

Proverbs 8:24

Before the mountains were settled, before the hills was I brought forth.

Proverbs 8:25

While as yet he had not made the earth, nor the fields, nor the highest part of the dust of the world.

Proverbs 8:26

Who is the image of the invisible God, the first-born of every creature:

Colossians 1:15

For by him were all things created, that are in heaven, and that are in earth, visible and invisible, whether they be thrones, or dominions, or principalities, or powers: all things were created by him, and for him.

Colossians 1:16

And he is before all things, and by him all things consist.

Colossians 1:17

And there shall come forth a rod out of the stem of Jesse, and a Branch shall grow out of his roots.

Isaiah 11:1

And the child grew, and waxed strong in spirit, filled with wisdom: and the grace of God was upon him.

Luke 2:40